Lisa Lintott

Going for Gold

Salamander Street

PLAYS

First published in 2024 by Salamander Street Ltd., a Wordville imprint. (info@salamanderstreet.com).

Going for Gold © Lisa Lintott, 2024

Cover photo by Andres Reynaga

Photo of Frankie Lucas, 10th April 1979, at a London gym, by Central Press/ Getty Images.

ISBN: 9781068696275

10 9 8 7 6 5 4 3 2 1

Further copies of this publication can be purchased from www.salamanderstreet.com

Wordville

ACKNOWLEDGEMENTS

This play is dedicated to my exceptionally talented children: Sidney Sunshine and Jazzy Wazzy for just being really beautiful human beings and my greatest source of pride and joy.

To my family, those behind: Rose Hollingsworth, John Lintott, Wayne Lintott, Elliott Lintott and those in front: Zach, Johnny, Gemma, Grant and Julie.

It rests in memory of Frankie Lucas, Alex Bruce, Michael Grant, Karen Renders and, of course, my great mate Trevor Smith, and acknowledges it would have not been possible without the love and support of: Alan and Marcus, Marcello and Roberto, Liz and Gary, Tina and Dickie, Sasha and Georgia, Laura and Stan, the marvellous Frani and Sue, Esther, Neil and Synergy Theatre, Cat, Christine, Carlaa, the delightful Dacre, Danny, David, Ed Daffern, Dominque De Lite, Fiona, John Barkus, Lauralyn, Manjula, Marilyn, Manami, Peter Spark, Roger Barker, Gorgeous Jen, Tara and the girls, Joanne Evans, Lindsay, Sophie, Simon and all who loved me when I had no space to be loved.

Plus a heart felt thanks to those who showed the faith: The Chairman: Andrew Moore, Kevin and Char Givens, David McClafferty, Marissa LeStrade, Gareth Allen, Annette Russell, Cleo Hector, Michelle Ifilli-Jenkins, Jack Bedder Ken Birage, Shaun Cooke, Sanjay Gunaillaka, Rohit Kapoor, Hugo Ohito, James Madders and James Monk, British Vintage Boxing, Tom Kilgallon Shoes, Folk Clothing, London Ex-Boxers Association and Ringside Charitable Trust.

Special thanks to: Steve Bunce, Ken Rimmington, Tony Chapman, John Conteh, Winston and Clinton MacKenzie, Bunny Johnson, Bruce Baker and Daniel Francis for sharing the knowledge.

And the biggest love to: Gene and Michael Bovell for trusting me with the story.

Lisa Lintott
2024

Going for Gold was first produced at Rotunda Theatre, Brighton Fringe (Winner of the Fuse International Best Theatre Award) on 29th May 2023.

CAST

FRANKIE LUCAS | **JAZZ LINTOTT**

GENE | **LLEWELLA GIDEON**

GEORGE | **NIGEL BOYLE**

KEN | **CYRIL BLAKE**

MICHAEL | **DANIEL FRANCIS-SWABY**

ALTERNATE FRANKIE LUCAS | **TINASHE DARIKWA**

CREATIVES

WRITER | **LISA LINTOTT**

DIRECTORS | **PHILIP J MORRIS & XANTHUS**

PRODUCERS | **LISA LINOTT & JAZZ LINTOTT**

ASSOCIATE PRODUCERS | **FRANK SCULLY & BEL CLARKE**

CASTING DIRECTOR | **HARRY GILBERT**

PRODUCTION MANAGERS | **TIAN GLASGOW & HANNAH MOORE**

PRODUCTION DESIGNER | **ERIN GUAN**

LIGHTING DESIGNER | **CHENG KENG**

SOUND DESIGNER | **LO WU**

MOVEMENT DIRECTORS | **DAVID GILBERT & RUPERT CHARMAK**

TECH STAGE MANAGEMENT | **REUBEN BO JENG & EMMA LANGAN**

STAGE MANAGEMENT | **SHEREEN HAMILTON**

VIDEOGRAPHER | **ARCHIE MACDONALD & ERICA BELTON**

CREATIVE DIRECTOR | **DACRE BRACEY**

DIALECT COACH | **JOEL TRILL**

PHOTOGRAPHERS | **ANDRES REYNAGA & JAMES POTTER**

ABOUT THE CAST

Jazz Lintott | FRANKIE

Jazz is an actor based in the UK and Canada. He began acting as part of the National Youth Theatre and studied at Italia Conti. He went on to do a MA at the Royal Central School of Speech and Drama, graduating in 2019. Jazz's film and TV credits include featuring in *5lbs of Pressure* opposite Luke Evans; *Alien Uprising* opposite Jean Claude Van Damme; *Triassic Attack* opposite Emilia Clarke; and *Airborne* alongside Mark Hamil and Julian Glover. Jazz was a series regular in *The Real Hustle* for two seasons and featured in ITV's *Emmerdale*. Awards include Best Male Lead in a Play, Best Producer and Best Production at the Black British Theatre Awards in 2023 for his involvement in *Going for Gold*.

Llewella Gideon | GENE

Llewella's theatre credits include *Faith, Hope and Charity* (Alexander Zeldin Company); *Under the Sun* (Royal Court); *Marys Seacole* (Donmar Warehouse); *The Long Song* (Chichester Festival Theatre); *Play Mas* by Mustafa Matura (Orange Tree Theatre); *The Vote* (Donmar Warehouse); *The Best of the Little Big Woman*; (Dual Impact Productions); *Family Man* (Theatre Royal Stratford East) and *Birthday* (Royal Court). Film credits include *Rye Lane; Harry Hill The Movie, Second Coming; Before I Go To Sleep; Nativity* and *Manderlay*. TV credits include *Eastenders* (BBC); *Mr Loverman* (BBC); *Boarders* (BBC); *Queenie* (Channel 4); *Gangsta Granny Strikes Again; Small Axe: Mangrove* (BBC); Gameface (Channel 4); *Trigonometry* (BBC) and *Absolutely Fabulous* (BBC).

Nigel Boyle | GEORGE

Nigel's theatre credits include *How Love is Spelt* (Southwark Playhouse); *A Dybbuk* (Crescent Theatre); *Circus Land* (New Leicester Square Theatre); *If Music Be The Food of Love* (Bankhaous Theatre) and *Sweet Love Remembered* (Shakespeare's Globe). Film credits include *Alleycats; Une Rencontre; Young High and Dead* and *The Best Years*. TV credits include *High Hoops* (BBC); *Three Little Birds* (ITV); *Sister Boniface Mysteries* (BBC); *Line of Duty* (BBC/Netflix); *Small Axe* (BBC/Amazon); *Silent Witness* (BBC); *The End of the F**king World* (Netflix); *Hetty Feather* (BBC); *Peaky Blinders; Humans* (Channel 4); *Coronation Street* (ITV); *Emmerdale* (ITV); *Doctors* (BBC) and *Peep Show*.

Cyril Blake | KEN

Cyril Blake is a regular on the Fringe theatre circuit and has recently been touring his one-person show *Bonding*, a semi-autobiographical account about learning that you don't have to be what people expect you to be. Having been raised in a rural mining village in Yorkshire, he thrives on telling the stories of the working class and under represented people and their struggle against adversity. He has also appeared in the BAFTA winning short film *Black Cop* and the audio drama series *Persons of Interest*, exploring the lives of black and queer artists. He has grown a moustache especially for the role of Ken Rimington in *Going for Gold*.

Daniel Francis-Swaby | MICHAEL

Micheal's theatre credits include *The Book of Grace* (Arcola Theatre); *Little Women* (HOME Theatre) and *Going for Gold* (Chelsea Theatre). Film and TV credits include *Rumplestiltskin; Alex Rider; Small Axe* (BBC) and *London's Knife Wars: What's The Solution* (BBC).

Tinashe Darikwa | FRANKIE LUCAS (ALTERNATE)

Tinashe's theatre credits include *Community Service* (Stan's Cafe); *Cuffed* (Theatre503); *Small Island* (Inspire Academy) and *Diary of a Football Nobody* (Etcetera Theatre). Film and TV credits include *Sherwood S2* (BBC); *Fourth to the Floor* (Channel 4); *Time Keeps Ticking, Hamster* and *Goodbye*.

ABOUT THE CREATIVES

Philip J Morris | Co-Director

Philip J Morris is the Artistic Director at Trybe House Theatre and a practitioner and grime historian. He studied a BA (Hons) in Applied Theatre at the Royal Birmingham Conservatoire. He has directed work for the Royal Shakespeare Company, Residenz Theatre (Munich), Young Vic, Bush Theatre, Soho Theatre, Southbank Centre, New Diorama Theatre, The Rep, and Talawa. Credits include: *Before I Go* (Brixton House); *Sitting In Limbo* (Watford Palace Theatre); *Romeo & Juliet* (Royal Shakespeare Company); *Manorism* (Southbank Centre); *Bitches* (Residenz Theatre); *Of The Cut* (Young Vic); *Clutch* (Bush Theatre); *Sessions* (Paines Plough); *18* (New Diorama); *Neighbourhood Voices* (Young Vic). Film Directing: *Recovery In Vision* (Tea Films); *Living Newspaper Editions* (Royal Court). Audio Plays: *Copper & Lead* (BBC Radio 4); *The Holding 'GNR8'* (LAMDA).

Xanthus | Co-Director

Xanthus' director credits: *When It Snows In April* (Streatham Space Project); *Galentine's Day* (Omnibus Theatre); *Big House; Big House* (Royal Central School of Speech and Drama); *If I Could Love; Just Nod* and *Repossession* (Theatre 503); *Black Joy* (Almeida Theatre). Director of the audio play *Ep 4–Erica* for the *Hear Myself Think* Podcast. Resident Director of *An Inspector Calls* UK/ Ireland tour.Assisting credits: *Changing Destiny* (The Young Vic); *Dear Elizabeth* (The Gate); *PYNEAPPLE* (The Bunker Theatre); *I Don't Care* (National Youth Theatre). Movement Director credits: *When It Snows In April* (Streatham Space Project); *Back to Oz* (Royal Central School of Speech and Drama); *Dust on a Mirror is Kin* (NDT Broadgate). Writing credits: *Up All Night* (Duke of York Theatre) and *Origins: Identity* (The Bush Theatre). Film credits: Director of *Posters* (Mountview); Assistant Director of *A Moment's Peace* (Hope Theatre). Photography featured: The Outernet, TimeOut magazine, The Guardian.

Harry Gilbert | Casting Director

Harry is one of the UK's most exciting up and coming casting directors. *Going for Gold* is Harry's first play as a Casting Director. His first feature *Reawakening* stars Jared Harris, Juliet Stevenson and Erin Doherty and was released in the UK and Ireland to critical acclaim. His first TV show as Casting Director was *G'WED* (ITVX), within two months of its February release it became the most watched comedy across ITV channels since 2020 and secured a further commission for a Series 2 and 3. As Casting Director: *G'WED* (ITVX); *Great Brittons* (Channel 4 pilot); *LIONS* (BIFA nominated 1st prize at Cannes 2023), *The Wasp, Underside, The Painting and The Statue, Home, Needleteeth, My Father Breaks Things, I'm Affraid of You.* Co-Casting for TV: *Truth and Conviction* (Angel Studios). As Casting Associate: *Lockerbie; Flight 103* (Sky and Peacock to be released in 2025), *Belgravia The Next Chapter* (MGM Plus). As Casting Assistant: *RRR* (Netflix), *Hotel Portafino* (PBS and ITV), *Suspect* (Channel 4), *The Control Room* (Hartswood Films and BBC).

Erin Guan | Production Designer

Erin Guan is a London-based scenographer, video designer and interactive installation artist from China. Her work spans intercultural performances and minority voices. Her recent theatre credit include *Going for Gold* (Come and Gold & Park Theatre); *The Dao of Unrepresentative British Chinese Experience* (Kakilang & Soho Theatre); *Romeo and Juliet* (Beats & Elements & Polka Theatre); *Turandot* (The Opera Makers & Ellandar & Arcola Theatre); *Pied*

Piper (Battersea Arts Centre); *The Apology* (New Earth Theatre & Arcola Theatre); *A Gig for Ghost* (Forty Five North & Soho Theatre Upstairs); *Unchain Me* (Dreamthinkspeak & Brighton Festival); *The Lonesome Death of Eng Bunker* (Kakilang x Omnibus Theatre); *Prayer for the Hungry Ghost* (Barbican Open Lab); *Foxes* (Defibrillator Theatre & Theatre 503); *Tokyo Rose* (Burnt Lemon Theatre). Her recent TV work include costume design for *East Mode S2* with Nigel Ng (Comedy Central & Channel 5).

Cheng Keng | Lighting Designer

Cheng Keng is a scenographer, lighting and video designer based in London. He trained at Royal Central School of Speech and Drama, completing an MFA in Scenography. Theatre credits include: *The Lonesome Death of Eng Bunker* (Omnibus Theatre); *Frankenstein* and *Rain Weaver* (Both Cockpit); *Grud* (Hampstead Theatre); *Grills* (CPT); *Project Atom Boi* and *So That You May Go Beyond The Sea* (All CPT); *1884* (Shoreditch Town Hall); *The Littlest Yak* (Marlowe studio); *Chriskirkpatrickmas* (Seven Dials Playhouse); *Tiger* (Omnibus Theatre); *555: Verlaine En Prison; Double Bill At the statue of Venus* and *La Voix Humaine* (Arcola); *1984* (The Cockpit); *Let Your Hands Sing In The Silence* (Marlowe Theatre); *these words that'll linger like ghosts till the day i drop down dead* (The Pleasance); *The Retreat* and *Pennyroyal* (Finborough); *The Zone* (Taoyuan Art Centre); *Sankofa: Before the Whitewash* (Roundhouse); *Beauty and the 7 Beasts* (Brixton Jamm); *Borders* (Drayton Arms Theatre); *Blue Island 99* (International Dublin Gay Theatre Festival) and *Hello World* (National Taichung Theatre, Taiwan).

Lo-Wu | Sound Designer

Lo-Wu is a Sound Designer, Composer, Music Producer and DJ and South London native. With a passion for storytelling and world-building through sound across music, film and theatre—blending styles and themes, uncovering musicality within naturalism. Theatre Credits: *Going for Gold* (Park Theatre); *Snakes & Ladders* (Southwark Playhouse); *Bougie Lanre's Boulangerie* (Talawa); *Love in Gravitational Waves* (Talawa); *FOAM* (Finborough Theatre); *What I Hear I Keep* (Talawa—TYPT 2023).

Sidders | Original Scores

Hailing from Kilburn, northwest London, Sidders entered music alongside Natty Wylah, Carl Blarx and K the infinite, as a vocalist and producer on *Wisdom of My Youth*. Since then, releases such as the bedroom EP *About Time* and more recently *May Snow* and *Better Days* have drawn over 1.5 million streams and parallels to inspirations such as Sampha, Tom Misch and

Loyle Carner. In between hip-hop, soul and indie it's an alternative style that brings ease to any listening,

David Gilbert | Movement Director

Theatre credits include, as Director: *Cups on a String* (Riding Lights, UK tour); *Another Star To Steer By* (Brighton Festival); *Parallel The Convert Zimbabwe*, *Umtolo* (Young Vic); *Windrush Time Capsule* (Africa Centre); *Disney Dysfunction* (Assembly Rooms, Edinburgh); *Voices* (Theatre 503); *Privileges* (Young Vic); *It's A O* (Union Theatre and Cambridge Junction); *Mapping Brent* (Kiln Theatre); and *TAH: The African Heterosexual* (AE Harris). As Associate Director: *Metamorphosis* (Frantic Assembly, Theatre Royal Plymouth, Curve, MAST Mayflower Studios and Lyric Hammersmith Theatre) and *Othello* (Frantic Assembly and Leicester Curve Tour). As Movement Director: *We All Know How This Ends* (Royal Stratford East). As Assistant Director: *Ticking* (Trafalgar Studios); *SESSIONS* (Paines Plough and Soho Tour); *Dennis of Penge* (Oval House and The Albany); *All Stones All Sides* (Young Vic); *A Season In The Congo* (Young Vic) and *Parallax* (Almeida Theatre). As Co-Director: *The Trials* (Marlowe, Kent) and *tyroneisaacstuart presents S!CKnotes* (BAC). Films include: *Tales From The Front Line* (Talawa) and *The Magnificent Life of Claudia Jones* (Unicorn).

Rupert Charmak | Fight Director

Rupert is an award-winning writer/ director, actor and fight director for screen and stage and the founder of Suckerpunch Productions. *I AM SUPER*, his recent short film, is a semi-finalist at BAFTA & Oscar-qualifying Rhode Island International Film Festival. *Dark Justice*, his first film as writer/director won best human rights film and best international at Atlantic Bridge Film Festival in Amsterdam. Rupert was a fight coordinator on *The Effects of Lying* on ITVX, *The Pebble and The Boy* on Amazon and he has worked on Season 2 and 3 of *Grave* with ITV. Rupert recently finished directing the play *Punchlines*, starring BAFTA-winning actor Brian Capron.

Joel Trill | Dialect Coach

Joel trained as a voice coach at The Royal Central School of Speech and Drama, where he was awarded the VASTA Diversity Scholarship. His extensive experience working with a variety of actors, allows him to be responsive, intuitive and adaptable as a coach. Joel has been co-running the Diaspora Accents For Actors (DAFA) Workshops, which specify in accents ranging from the Caribbean to North, East, West and Southern

African regions. Joel has also coached on a variety of urban and multi-ethnic British and American accents. His specialism in this variety of accents has led to coaching Oscar-Nominated artists.

Jazz Lintott | Producer

Jazz Lintott is currently a Stage One Producer Bursary recipient. He is also a professional actor with a diverse background in film and theatre. He began his producing career at Shimmer Films, working on music videos for artists such as Giggs, N-Dubz and Toploader. Transitioning to feature films, he collaborated with industry legends like Stan Lee, Jason Mewes and Danny Trejo. Jazz made his theatre producing debut with *Going for Gold*, which earned him and the team the Best Producer and Best Play awards at the 2023 Black British Theatre Awards.

Lisa Lintott | Producer

Lisa Lintott has a background in education, media and journalism. This is her debut play and debut production. Written in part for her son and as a recollection of her childhood, *Going for Gold* was shortlisted for the RSC 37 Plays and won Fuse International Best Theatre Award at Brighton Fringe 2023 and Best Play, Best Producer and Best Male Lead Actor at the Black British Theatre Awards 2023. Lisa is currently editing her first novel.

Frank Skully | Associate Producer

An award-winning writer and producer, Frank has worked with Synergy Theatre for over 12 years. His production credits include *SoundClash the Musical* at Edinburgh Fringe 2023 and *Going for Gold*, for which he shared the Best Producer award and Best Play Award at the Black British Theatre Award 2023.

Tian Glasgow | Production Manager

Tian Glasgow (he/him) is a queer cis Black man. He grew up in London but has lived in Manchester since 2019. He founded the theatre company New Slang Productions in 2011. The thread running through his work as a theatre director are social concerns such as race and class and how it affects communities. He teaches acting at ALRA, MMU and LIPA. Outside this, Tian is a Senior Creative Producer of theatre, arts and music events. Previously working on Fertility Fest, Walthamstow Garden Party, The Sick of the Fringe: Care and Destruction Festival, Love Supreme and London

Jazz Festival. For five years he has been the Manchester Programme Coordinator for Arts Emergency, a youth mentoring charity. Most recently, he completed his first year as the Royal Exchange Young Company Performers Lead directing the show *Threshold* and took up the new role of Programme Development Lead at Something to Aim For charity.

Hannah Moore | Production Manager

Hannah Moore is a freelance Production Manager currently working across the UK and New Zealand. Specialising in Performance Art, Theatre and large-scale events she is Head of Production for Festival of Live Art Auckland and Senior Production Manager for Assembly Festivals and Auckland Arts Festival . Her theatre work crosses a broad spectrum managing work including The Famous Lauren Bari Holstein, Split Britches, Julia Croft, Lizz Carr, Metis & Tim Crouch.

Shereen Hamilton | Stage Management

Shereen is a Creative Practitioner with a BA and MA in Theatre and Performance. Shereen has trained and worked as a producer, director, actor, stage manager and facilitator. Her area of work centres around intersectional identities on stage and using theatre as a vehicle of education. Credits include: Assistant Director on *seven methods of killing kylie jenner* (The Royal Court Theatre, May–July 2021); Director on Jamie Hale's *CRIPtic Pit Party* (The Barbican, Oct 2019), Producer on *#BlackIs* (Company Three / New Diorama, March–September 2023); Creative Producer on *SAMSKARA* (The Yard Theatre, July 2022); Stage Manager on Directors development R&D at Headlong Theatre; Stage Manager on *The Great Privation* (Theatre 503, May 2024) Community Connector on Artist Development Programme at Southbank Centre and Production Trainee on *Taskmaster* at Avalon Productions / Channel 4.

Dacre Bracey | Creative Director

A pluralist by nature, Dacre is an accomplished creative director and brand builder, whose work is born from a lifelong passion for street culture and music. He enjoys being surrounded by talented people and a culture of positivity, bravery and passion. He has worked with renowned brands and brilliant people on a broad range of prestigious projects.

Andres Reynaga | Photography

Born in Bogotó, Colombia, Andres' interest in photography began when he was studying advertising and design. He found in photography a great way of telling stories that lived inside his head. A few years later his passion turned into a professional photography career, leading him to work with major brands such as Oscar de la Renta and Mercedes Benz Fashion Week Panama. His storytelling is inspired by beauty and strength often portraying subjects with a romantic, yet strong and empowering character, making his cinematic style quite unique. Currently resides in Panama City, Panama and regularly travels for assignments, working between Panama City, Bogota and CDMX.

James Potter | Photography

James Potter is a rock and fashion photographer based in London, with a strong presence in the city's vibrant cultural scene. Born and raised in Croydon (where parts of this play take place) one of his first jobs was working on a documentary about boxing legend Duke McKenzie at his Crystal Palace gym. James currently studies at Central Saint Martins.

PARK THEATRE

ABOUT PARK THEATRE

Park Theatre was founded by Artistic Director, Jez Bond and Creative Director Emeritus, Melli Marie. The building opened in May 2013 and, with nine West End transfers, two National Theatre transfers and 15 national tours in its first ten years, quickly garnered a reputation as a key player in the London theatrical scene. Park Theatre has received seven Olivier nominations, won numerous Off West End Offie Awards, and won The Stage's Fringe Theatre of the Year and Accessible Theatre Award.

Park Theatre is an inviting and accessible venue, delivering work of exceptional calibre in the heart of Finsbury Park. We work with writers, directors and designers of the highest quality to present compelling, exciting and beautifully told stories across our two intimate spaces.

Our programme encompasses a broad range of work from classics to revivals with a healthy dose of new writing, producing in-house as well as working in partnership with emerging and established producers. We strive to play our part within the UK's theatre ecology by offering mentoring, support and opportunities to artists and producers within a professional theatre-making environment.

Our Creative Engagement strategy seeks to widen the number and range of people who participate in theatre, and provides opportunities for those with little or no prior contact with the arts.
In everything we do we aim to be warm and inclusive; a safe, welcoming and wonderful space in which to work, create and visit.

★★★★★ "A five-star neighbourhood theatre." Independent

As a registered charity [number 1137223] with no public subsidy, we rely on the kind support of our donors and volunteers. To find out how you can get involved visit parktheatre.co.uk

FOR PARK THEATRE

Artistic Director Jez Bond
Executive Director Catherine McKinney

Artistic

Producer & Programmer Amelia Cherry
Development & Producing Coordinator Ellen Harris

Creative Engagement

Creative Engagement Manager Carys Rose Thomas

Development

Head of Development Ama Ofori-Darko

Finance

Finance Director Elaine Lavelle
Finance Officer Nicola Brown
Finance Assistant Pinar Kurdik

General Management

General Manager Tom Bailey
Deputy General Manager David Hunter
Administrator Mariah Sayer
Duty Venue Managers Leiran Gibson, Zara Naeem, Laura Riseborough, Shaun Joyson, Wayne Morris, Amber De Ruyt

Park Pizza

Supervisors Luke Rogan & Toby Schuster
Team Members George Gehm, Bradly Doko, Hugo Harrison, Alex Kristoffy, Julia Skinner, Maddie Stoneman, Ruairi McGonagle, Saron Tariku, Harry Taylor, Athena Vlachos, Sion Watkins, Jessie Williams, Maria Ziolkowska

Lisa Lintott

Going for Gold

CHARACTERS

FRANKIE

Male, 20s—60s, a Middleweight boxer from St Vincent, part of the Windrush Generation, he came to England aged nine but never lost his accent. Strong silent type, sometimes considered moody as he does not suffer fools gladly or understand the play of politics. He is very well mannered and has a dry sharp wit. He wants recognition for his talent and a chance to succeed.

GENE

Female, 50s, Frankie's first love and mother to his son, from Barbados. She also came to the UK aged nine. She narrates the story as a knowing observer and protector understanding her and Frankie's limits. She has a razor tongue. Ultimately she just wants the best for herself and her son.

KEN

Male, 40s, an ambitious policeman from Derby, Ken runs the amateur boxing club where Frankie trained from age nine to 21. He is a father figure and promotes strong family values and authority. He wants the club and his lads to succeed—whatever it takes.

GEORGE

Male, 40s, a professional trainer. A salt-of-the-earth type of bloke. He has been round the houses and knows the pain of poverty. The first trainer to actively take on a stable of black boxers he is not afraid of fighting tooth and nail to get world champions. He is driven by a sense of justice and wants to make right the wrongs of his world.

MICHAEL

Male, 40s, an open and astute man, he is Frankie's son and only child. He looks after Frankie, caring for him, with a sense of duty and compassion for his father's troubled story. He admires his father but he wants acceptance and acknowledgement as a man in his own right.

SETTING

We are in London. In a boxing gym. The ring is centre stage—it is basic—there are four small wooden stools in each corner and a microphone hanging down in the centre of the stage. A screen is suspended behind the ring—almost like a wall or curtain. Outside the ring—to the left of the stage is an old sofa and lamp and to the right of the stage is a Regency-style reproduction mahogany desk with green leather inlay. A phone sits on it.

TIME

We travel from the late 60s to 2023.

This script represents the play at the time of rehearsal and there could be changes during the production.

ACT ONE

SCENE 1

The Sir Philip Game Boys Club in Croydon.

It is late afternoon. A hazy dusty yellow hue saturates the gym.

A Pathe Newsreel from 1948 "Copper Socking School" plays on the projector.

KEN in his police constable's uniform walks onto the stage and over to the desk— he looks around beaming a smile as he holds a set of keys—the projector now reads: "1968".

KEN picks up the phone and dials a number.

KEN: Ray? You ready to train? It's great! I.... We can do this. I can feel it.

He listens and smiles as he looks around at the ring and punching bag centre-stage.

A young boy (FRANKIE) walks in from the left hand side of the stage. He walks quietly and nervously past the sofa, then the boxing apparatus, to reach the desk. Ken is watching him whilst listening.

KEN: I'll see you Saturday then.

He puts down the phone.

Allo, Allo, Allo—what have we got here?

FRANKIE hangs his head.

Have you come to box?

FRANKIE: Yes, Sir.

KEN: What's your name?

FRANKIE: Frankie.

KEN: How old are you?

FRANKIE: Nine, Sir.

KEN: Well, Frankie, you'll need to come back when you're 11.

FRANKIE: But me stronger dan 11.

He holds his arms up to show his muscles.

FRANKIE: Jump pan me—me hold still. Me nah cry! Cry-cry baby, nah geh no rights.

FRANKIE stands firm, eyes shut.

KEN: (*laughs*) It's nothing personal, just the rules.

FRANKIE: Me need to come now, Sir.

KEN: Oh, you do, do you?

FRANKIE looks at him straight in the eyes and nods.

KEN: But the rules are the rules. They say you need to be 11 to get into that ring and there's nothing I can do about that. And as time waits for no man, Frankie, you'll have to run along.

FRANKIE stays put and just stares at KEN with a certain need in his eyes. KEN looks at him a little baffled.

KEN: Do you know what it takes to become a great boxer Frankie?

FRANKIE shrugs his shoulders.

KEN: Listening and doing, doing everything you're told.

FRANKIE: (*Still not going anywhere*) Me do everything me told.

KEN: So run along then.

KEN shoos him out

FRANKIE remains unmoved and adds quickly before Ken can say anything else...

FRANKIE: But me fight better.

FRANKIE does a little shuffle and punch.

KEN gives a little chuckle.

KEN: You do know fighting and boxing are two different things?

FRANKIE: How so?

KEN: One is done with temper out of the ring and the other with skill inside the ring.

(Beat.)

FRANKIE: De rules stop I from watching?

KEN: No, I can't say they do. There are no rules on watching.

FRANKIE: So me caan come den?

KEN looks at the boy with intrigue and then smiles.

KEN: Why not?

FRANKIE: Tank you, Sir.

FRANKIE smiles.

KEN goes to ruffle his hair but stops when FRANKIE moves half-a-step back and flinches at KEN's movement—so KEN pulls his arm back.

KEN: Where's that accent from, Frankie?

FRANKIE: St Vincent, Sir.

KEN: Well, young Frankie from St Vincent, we open for business on Saturday. Two days from now. Come at nine, don't be late. Ray hates lateness.

FRANKIE: Who Ray is?

KEN: Who Ray is? Oh, who Ray is—Ray is the trainer.

FRANKIE: Yo nah train we?

KEN: No, I run the club, get the matches. You'll see. Nine sharp and get your father to bring you.

FRANKIE: Me Mummy caan come?

KEN: Yes, your Mother can come.

BLACK OUT.

SCENE 2

The projector shows 1971.

Johnny Reggae *by The Piglets plays.*

> *A woman is on the sofa. She is around 50+, black and from Barbados. She stands up to address the audience.*

GENE: I'm not his mother, by the way. If that's what you're thinking. No, I'm Gene, his son's mother.

GENE sings along to Johnny Reggae then stops to continue.

GENE: Yes, it's 1971. I'm 15 and Frankie Lucas is going on 17 and too sweet then: Sporting his big afro, one of them slick two-tone suit, with the trouser crease so starched, it's like the trousers wear him; oh, and the white crisp cutaway collar of his cotton shirt sitting on his lapels like angel wings, ready to carry him proud and strong.

(Beat and a smile.)

Like a king. He walks like he don't suffer fools gladly, not one, and he don't say much, but one of his side-eye looks sees right through you and cuts you sharper than a knife.

FRANKIE enters, comes over and grabs her.

And to me, he's that fine, he makes my knees go weak.

Girl of My Dreams *by Cornel Campbell plays.*

GENE (CONTD): (*Giggles*) And as my Mummy used to say "every moldy bread hav' it moldy cheese" We start 'seeing' each other. Meeting on our 'likkle bench' spending hours talking 'bout back home' and wondering why the hell we both got sent for, to this cold country, where I work the hardest for the least wage.

FRANKIE: And I win the schoolboy Championship AND the Junior ABA but dem nah give me no crown.

GENE: Coz nothin' in Inglan mek sense to we.

(beat)

And when day turns to night we fill our hungry bellies full at the Wimpy and quench our thirst at The Swan pub in Penge, where Graham the DJ likes reggae.

FRANKIE: And I like to dance.

He pulls her towards him and they dance.

GENE: Before you see me on the bus home.

FRANKIE: With the weekly bus pass I get you.

GENE smiles at him and then looks to the audience

GENE: And well before you know it, I sweet 16, Frankie going on 18 and I get catch.

GENE rubs her belly.

FRANKIE: By a world champion.

GENE: And him so front-page, who am I to doubt him?

GENE sits back down on the sofa

The light switches to KEN.

KEN is behind the desk in a formal navy suit and tie. He has obviously gone up in the world.

KEN is on the phone watching FRANKIE shadow box. FRANKIE is focused and working with steely determination.

KEN: It's a shame, but it is what it is.

Beat as KEN listens.

I understand that YOU have plans in place but my Frankie is an awkward strong bugger, and let's face it, boxing IS his ONLY talent.

(Beat.)

NO. I won't handle him like that, Mr. Duff He's about to give your golden boy a run for his money and I tell you what I'm betting on mine winning and if I were you I'd do the same—

KEN laughs, puts the phone down and stands outside the ring to speak to FRANKIE.

You're looking good, Frankie.

FRANKIE nods, stops and climbs out of the ring.

KEN: You can beat Minter but it won't be an easy fight.

FRANKIE: Easy ain't a fight.

FRANKIE gives KEN a wink.

KEN: Be warned he doesn't travel light and his crowd is tough.

FRANKIE: Me nah study the crowd.

KEN: Even at the Royal Albert Hall?

FRANKIE: Where?

FRANKIE gently punches KEN's arm.

KEN: Minter's odds on favourite, but win this Frankie and the ABA will be yours.
You confident enough to get your gal to have a little flutter?

FRANKIE: And have you arrest her? You forget she only 16, it's her sister that 18.

FRANKIE smiles.

FRANKIE's playing KEN. FRANKIE looks directly at KEN.

They both smile.

FADES TO BLACK.

SCENE 3

The projector shows 1972.

Feel the Spirit*: The Ethiopians plays.*

FRANKIE punches the punch bag as he picks up his towel and walks away to the sofa.

GENE: Michael came with the sheet rain in January and gale-force winds followed him in February

FRANKIE gets to the sofa and sits down, rolls a spliff then gently rocks a Moses basket housing Michael, his son.

The chorus of The Ethiopians' Feel the Spirit *plays.*

Twinkle Twinkle Little Star *plays.*

FRANKIE: *(softly)* Don't fret, Michael. You'll never go hungry or stand the cold alone.

FRANKIE gets up and leaves to go back to the gym

GENE: Frankie's fight with Minter was on the 29th March. He trained so hard not the storms nor the bitter cold could slow him down. We didn't see him for dust and if, God forbid, I needed to reach him...

(Beat.)

I felt like an outside woman begging for his time.

FRANKIE: Boxing and women don't mix.

GENE: So I put up and shut up.

FRANKIE: And came to watch me anyway.

GENE: *(To the audience)* A ringside seat at the Royal Albert Hall and, as we'd been getting by on just my little wage for three months now, and I'd never been, I went to see what all the fuss was about.
You should have seen me getting ready, I was all fingers and thumbs.

FRANKIE: Wearing the red coat I bring for you.

GENE: A beautiful coat. Pure wool with big black buttons and hand-stitched buttonholes. And the red dress you had my mother tailor for me.

FRANKIE: With the lace cuffs.

GENE: I style a small neat afro.

She pats her hair.

Like yours Frankie.

(She looks back to the audience) And my sister gave me her gold loop earrings and, if I say so myself, I was like Cinderella going to the ball, except outside it raining cats and dogs and my carriage was the 159 bus.

FRANKIE: And my name on the poster welcomed you.

GENE: It did. And, like a Queen, I walked into my palace.

FRANKIE: *(Smiles)* To a sea of foaming mouth sharks.

GENE: To sit with the South London warrior Mackenzie Brothers.

FRANKIE: Your black face and theirs making six in the whole crowd.

GENE: But when you came and climbed into that ring...

FRANKIE climbs into the ring-stands by the ropes and looks at GENE.

GENE: So sure of yourself—you plastered a smile on my face not a mountain or the Devil himself could move.

FRANKIE smiles.

FRANKIE: You catch me eye.

FRANKIE nods and smiles at GENE and then goes to his corner.

GENE: And both of us beam with pride.

FRANKIE: No-one gonna take away our night.

The bell rings.

FRANKIE walks tall to the middle of the ring.

FRANKIE: Yeah, man.

GENE: Victory sitting on him tighter than his gloves.

RING ANNOUNCER (V/O): Round One.

GENE looks into the ring.

Crowd noise sounds.

GENE: Hear that? The whole damn place erupting for Minter but Frankie don't care. He's bringing the tornado and when Frankie ducks his fist...

The crowd boos with hostilities.

Frankie goes full force and in no time at all between the dancing, the heads clashing, and Frankie's left hook, Minter gets a real bad deep cut and it so fast the Ref has no choice but to end it

FRANKIE: Less than two minutes.

GENE: Typical Frankie.

GENE smirks with innuendo.

KEN raises FRANKIE's arm in triumph and they both smile.

FRANKIE looks straight at GENE and winks—GENE jumps out of her seat arms up in the air.

GENE: YES, FRANKIE!!!

The crowd's boos and chants for Minter make GENE sit down.

GENE (CONTD): *(Back to the audience)* But when that crowd saw Minter's blood streaming down his face, it's like they came for Frankie's in return. The nastiness that crowd screamed slid down my neck, down my back and my legs to reach my feet til I jump up and sprint up that aisle dodging those ugly Union Jack-waving bodies faster than Ivory Crockett. Faster than Frankie won the fight. And I never stopped running til I reach the bus stop I arrived at, like it Switzerland, sat quiet, almost invisible on my lonesome til them lot came find me to carry me home.

FRANKIE: *(Laughs)* Thats' just the way things run. Come let we go.

GENE: Where?

FRANKIE: The Q Club. We celebrating.

Lights go down and come up in the office.

KEN is behind the desk and FRANKIE is with him.

KEN goes to give him the paper but stops and points to the article instead.

KEN: The papers are calling you ferocious. It reports you cut Minter's eye in a savage attack he didn't see coming.

FRANKIE looks down at the papers on KEN's desk.

FRANKIE: Well, he definitely can't see it now.

FRANKIE and KEN both smile.

KEN: This is no laughing matter, Frankie.

FRANKIE: No? You didn't say "Well done, Frankie—you fought a bloody good fight" counting your winnings?

The phone rings.

KEN picks it up and looks at it as someone is shouting down the phone at him

KEN: Boxers tend to get hurt in fights. It's unfortunate but it is what it is. He'll get over it.

He listens further.

Is that it? We're all busy people and I'm sure you've got places to be, people to see—

KEN puts the phone down and looks at FRANKIE.

KEN: Tricky bugger.

FRANKIE: You frighten?

KEN: No. But don't pick fights with the wrong people.

FRANKIE: I don't pick the fights. You do.

KEN: Quite and if you win the ABA, an Olympic gold medal could be up for grabs. Imagine that, Frankie. Your talent can't go to waste so can you do as you're told...

FRANKIE: *(Ends his sentence for him)* ...and just keep listening? Nothing gonna stop we.

KEN: Ay. Your mouth to God's ears Frankie—your mouth to God's ears.

Lights go down and come back up on GENE.

GENE: So Frankie put his head down and sailed through the semi-finals in Manchester onto the final at Wembley. I told myself: Gal if you can't beat 'em join 'em and I carried myself to the storm: Same red coat and dress, same white crowd. Only this time I knew to sit firm in the middle of the Mackenzie Brothers like I was a soldier on the frontline, ready to watch my "Wild Man of the Ring."

The bell rings.

Boos and shouts / profanities are heard.

GENE: And Frankie, like he can't hear that noise, dances to the centre, like he's at The Q Club.

FRANKIE walks confidently back to the corner.

A bell rings.

RING ANNOUNCER (V/O): Round One.

GENE: Just look at how great MY Frankie is looking.

KEN: Jab, jab, light on your feet, pull him in—that's it, beautiful. Control the storm, Frankie, wait for your moment.

A bell rings twice.

RING ANNOUNCER (V/O): Round Two.

GENE: You can do it, Frankie.

KEN: That's it, Frankie, now take the fight to him.

A bell rings twice.

FRANKIE sits back in the corner.

RING ANNOUNCER (V/O): Round Three.

FRANKIE walks back to the centre.

KEN: Release that killer left hook and let's go home.

GENE: And he did. The Mackenzie family are laughing like hyenas and even if my feet felt to spring me up like a jack-in-the-box, once bitten twice shy, I stay rooted in my seat.

FRANKIE: Your eyes sparkling like cat's eyes in the dark.

KEN is in the ring,

KEN holds up FRANKIE's arm, KEN pats FRANKIE on the back. They laugh together, then FRANKIE winks at GENE

GENE: Because you, Frankie Lucas, my king man on May 5th 1972 at Wembley Arena, with a small smile on your face and me in the crowd, took your ABA crown.

FRANKIE: Not long now, Gene. Our treasures soon come.

FADES TO BLACK.

SCENE 4

KEN, who is in the office, going through some papers with agitation. He is nervous and then looks out to FRANKIE skipping, looking fit, happy and unbeatable.

Young, Gifted and Black *by Bob and Marcia plays.*

KEN comes out from the office, walks up to the radio and turns it off.

KEN: You know full well we don't train to music.

KEN goes back into the office. KEN picks up the phone then puts it down again, sits at his desk and then gets back up and goes out to FRANKIE.

FRANKIE looks at him.

KEN: When you're done can we have a word in my office?

KEN turns and walks back into his office slowly and uncomfortably,

FRANKIE winding down watches KEN and climbs out of the ring to follow him.

FRANKIE stands in the office looking at KEN.

KEN: I wanted to talk to you about the Olympics.

FRANKIE: My bag pack?

KEN: They haven't selected you.

FRANKIE: Them Who?

KEN: The Olympic Select Committee.

FRANKIE: They forget I'm British ABA champion?

KEN: Ay, they know alright.

FRANKIE just looks at Ken waiting for an explanation.

FRANKIE: You spit it out so easy?

KEN: Well, there's no easy way to say it. And before you say 'owt, Billy Knight's going in your place so it's not about you being coloured.

FRANKIE: Billy Knight's a light heavyweight.

KEN: Minter's going as the light heavyweight.

FRANKIE: Why?

KEN: Better odds for winning a medal. If you went as a middleweight and won gold it would rank you higher than Minter and upset the applecart if you both turned pro at the same time.

FRANKIE: Them wrong and strong so?

KEN looks quizzically at FRANKIE.

KEN: They're not taking any chances. And as the British Boxing Board of Control sit in Mr Duff's pockets and they lead the Select Committee we're buggered.

FRANKIE just looks at KEN processing the information. FRANKIE is clearly vexed and is waiting for more from KEN. KEN isn't forthcoming.

KEN: There is a silver lining. We get some time

FRANKIE: For what?

KEN: To get experience—like boxing in a country away from home

FRANKIE: I already away from home.

KEN: You know what I mean. All the media attention, I mean you're still so young, only 17.

FRANKIE: 18.

KEN: What?

FRANKIE: I'm 18. Ali got gold at 18, Conteh at 19.

KEN: But you've not had any international fights and you need to be ready for interviews...

FRANKIE: (*interrupts*) ...I going to Munich not Hollywood.

KEN: You know I couldn't go.

FRANKIE: But Ray could and I'd be part of the English Team.

KEN: Time is on our side.

FRANKIE: But MY time is now.

KEN: Alright, calm down. You know you have to be 21 to hold a British title, and you're still only 17.

FRANKIE: I 18. Ken.

KEN: Good things come to those that wait, think about it. Did you know I started working down the pits at 15?

FRANKIE shakes his head.

KEN: You ever been down the pits, Frankie? No? Course you haven't. Bloody vile places but when I was 17, like you now...

FRANKIE: I 18.

KEN: There was a problem with the pit tugs.

FRANKIE looks bemused.

FRANKIE: What they is?

KEN: Pit tugs? They carry the coal. They run on railway runners controlled by an inch and a half thick rope that goes round a return wheel. Anyway, the return wheel had broken.

(Beat.)

KEN waits for FRANKIE to acknowledge him but FRANKIE doesn't so he continues.

I was sent with a couple of lads to fix it, so we took it off and turned the engine off, but that meant the coal had to be moved by hand, hard bloody work, the kinda hard work that never leaves you, work like you'd never know.

FRANKIE: You do know I'm from the Caribbean?

KEN: Paradise. Anyway some silly prat thought he knew better and decided to start back the engine, but because there was no wheel to control it the rope flapped about.

FRANKIE: What was wrong with that?

KEN: I'll tell you what was wrong with that. It caught the man in front of me and in one fell swoop whipped his head straight off.

FRANKIE: You witnessed that?

KEN: He was closer to me than you are now. And the worse of it was we had to work the shift with the corpse and head lying there beside us. It took forever before someone came to bag the poor sod up.

(Beat.)

FRANKIE: What did you do?

KEN: I got outta there as fast as I could and ran to the Navy office at Chesterfield.

FRANKIE: Why? You like uniforms?

KEN: No, but it seemed an easy way out and even if Skegness ain't St Vincent, looking out to sea, I knew I'd go and never look back. Just like you now.

FRANKIE: Me nah run away, we was invited 'ere.

KEN: But the point is... The man told me to come back in four months. I was 17 and eight months old and the rules said I had to be 18. Anyhow I drove down to Portsmouth and got myself a little job waiting for the four months to pass. And then just as I signed up I was on the beach when I met this beautiful woman on a day trip from London.

FRANKIE: Your wife?

KEN: Yes. Funny thing was I fell out of the frying pan into the fire. Because I bloody hated the Navy and I'd signed up for seven years. BUT I learnt to write letters, I learnt endurance and, best of all, I learnt boxing.

FRANKIE: You learnt boxing in the Navy?

KEN: I did—and it gave me a name I'll never forget. Stoker McClaren Mcdonglin, the only lad I ever lost to.

(Beat.)

The Navy rewarded me with my wife. And the boxing gave me this club. And this club gave me you. So we've all reaped the rewards, together.

FRANKIE: What rewards I reaping?

KEN: Just hold your horses for two more years.

FRANKIE: You know, Ken, men of my birth can only dream of your choices, even your worse ones.

(Beat.)

This *(he looks around)* is all I got and I won't give up an Olympic gold medal. Dem men there wanna back the wrong horse and shorten their odds by robbing me.

KEN: I'm asking you. You came in on my first day and you've grown up with me. We've done this together, and we should end it together, you've got time, you're still only...

FRANKIE walks and puts on Eighteen with a Bullet by *Derek Harriot. FRANKIE walks back to KEN.*

KEN: *(Smugly)* And like I said, you have to be 21 to hold a British title.

(Beat.)

I'll get you some international fights, decent press, another ABA and a gold medal at the Commonwealth Games, the club will be recognized, you'll be ready to go pro and leave here, leave me...

FRANKIE: We ain't going all the way together?

KEN: You going pro will be the end of us. You'll go off as a British title contender and, with the right handling, you'll go all the way. I promise I'll sort you out a good manager but it's my job to get this club flourishing. And I'm too good a policeman to leave the force and give up my pension. I mean I've got a wife and three kids to think about.

FRANKIE goes and turns the music off and stays centre stage at the back.

Light on GENE.

GENE: Like Frankie didn't have Michael and me to think about. And lucky for Ken's wife, she didn't have to do a three-hour round trip on four different buses to get her baby to nursery before work and lose her job along the way. She didn't have to run herself rugged waiting for the promise of milk or clothes or money or even a visit, God forbid a night out, because amateur boxing ain't paid. No. She sat in a nice house looking after her kids whilst her policeman husband bought home the bacon.
Frankie wasn't wearing the strain I was. And it didn't look good on me one likkle bit.

FRANKIE: I ain't wearing the strain?

GENE: There just ain't no room for the two of we to wear it together.

KEN is at his desk and is on the phone.

KEN: I dunno, Mr Duff. He's not gonna like it, but I can ask him, but that's all I will do.

KEN puts down the phone and stares in FRANKIE's direction for a moment.

KEN: Frankie? A minute please. I've got you a little money earner.

FRANKIE walks in and sits down.

FRANKIE: You have?

KEN: Ay. It's a boxing match at the National Sporting Club. You'll be the entertainment at a dinner cabaret. A nice payday only open to the great and the good. You know the drill.

FRANKIE: Who with?

KEN: Minter. But before you say no, they've promised the best of three.

(Beat.)

Should he win.

FRANKIE: Him win?

KEN: Yes, him win. It'll be just before the Olympics with the rematch just after, just before he goes pro. You don't have to tell me now. Think on it. Think what'll do for Gene and Michael.

FRANKIE leaves the office and the lights go down.

They Will Rob You *by John Holt plays.*

GENE is dancing round the sofa.

FRANKIE walks in. His eye is cut and he is holding a present

GENE: What happened to your eye Frankie?

FRANKIE: Work.

GENE: You had a match?

FRANKIE holds out the bag but GENE doesn't take it. She keeps looking at him.

FRANKIE: Look this for Michael. Open it.

GENE takes it and reluctantly opens it and holds a baby's shirt in her hands.

GENE: It pretty, pretty.

FRANKIE: Twelve pounds pretty.

He smiles.

GENE: Twelve pounds?! Are you right in the head?

FRANKIE: It my Mother's birthday and I want Michael look nice.

GENE: £12. You know the whole heap of outfits that buy down East Street?

FRANKIE: You said Michael need new clothes.

GENE: Clothes. Not one shirt. I real vexed. So much on so little...

(Beat.)

Wait. You fought? I thought we discussed that. Please tell me you win?

FRANKIE: Minter get the better of me in the last round, but I'll catch him in the rematch.

GENE: You foolish. What rematch? Minter's got everything to lose in a rematch and you everything to gain.

FRANKIE turns and walks away aggresively, his back to GENE to exit.

GENE (CONTD): Close the lights and the door on your way out.

GENE turns to the audience

We turn on the Olympics to watch Billy Knight get knocked out early, Minter win Bronze, and him turn pro before he stepped off that blasted podium to rob my Frankie of his rematch. The whole thing itched Frankie's spirit worse than a swarm of damn mosquitoes buzzing round his ear ready to bite him, because he knew all he'd done was made right their wrong.

But I couldn't tell him nothing worth hearing, not with them father figures telling him to "spend his days holding on" and his 'bredren' telling him to "spend his nights letting go" all of them bound together by the love of a sport fuelled on anger and hate.

FADES TO BLACK.

SCENE 5

The projector shows 1973.

KEN is at his desk. He's back on the phone and really agitated.

KEN: No. Not again. If you do this to him Me and MY club suffer...

KEN listens.

MY reputation? It's not like I got a queue of kids at the door This will kill the club stone dead. And I'm not having it...

(Beat.)

Look, we've played ball with you, we've kept our heads down and our mouths shut. He's fought all the matches as they've come, we've been to New York, Belgrade and Amsterdam and won. AND let's not forget he is the ABA Champion FOR THE SECOND TIME so HE's going to New Zealand by hook or by crook.

(Beat as KEN listens.)

IT IS personal. He's a lad in MY club...

(Beat as KEN listens again)

No, Mr Duff, I'm not ANNOYED I'm bloody livid. I gave my word so...

KEN just holds the receiver and looks at the phone

FRANKIE is in the ring but just listening and looking straight at KEN. He walks into the office and sits down.

FRANKIE: This is on you.

KEN: I know

FRANKIE: New Zealand have the only blows I taking.

FRANKIE stands up and leans on the desk. Then he stands and crosses his arms.

KEN: Look, they're saying you knocked Billy Knight spark out in the dressing room before a match and that could lose you your licence.

FRANKIE: What?

(Beat puts his arms down.)

A big shot policeman like yourself listen to that?

KEN: I know.

KEN is nervous—FRANKIE is still staring at him.

FRANKIE: This is still on you. How do you even fight in a dressing room? And besides I like Billy.

(Beat.)

FRANKIE sits back down.

KEN: Isn't Billy from the same place as you?

FRANKIE: No. He's from St Kitts and I'm from St Vincent.

KEN: Same difference. They both in the Commonwealth right?

FRANKIE: Yes please... and it's the Commonwealth Games.

A lightbulb moment as they both think the same thing.

KEN: Yes it is

FRANKIE: So if Inglan' don't want me or my gold medal St Vincent will.

They both smile.

KEN starts to go through papers on his desk, he looks up at FRANKIE and smiles.

KEN: Yes, I'm sure they will.

FRANKIE: *(Laughs)* St Vincent have a team going?

KEN: Well, they have now. There's more than one way to skin a cat, Frankie my son, and more than one road to Christchurch.

KEN picks up a directory and finds a number. He picks up the phone and dials.

KEN: Hello is that the East Caribbean Commission? Yes, it is brilliant—Can I please speak to the Commissioner? Yes, it's Ken Rimmington, Chief Superintendent of Croydon Police and I have a proposition for you.

Lights shift to GENE.

GENE: And you know that Ken managed to set up a St Vincent Boxing Federation and make a late application via the Eastern Caribbean Commission to get it all approved in a few weeks. We all worked like Trojans to raise the money whilst Ken made sure Frankie trained like a champion.

FRANKIE is asleep on his sofa—a beer can and ashtray on the floor

A siren sounds.

A blue light flashes off-stage. The door is pounded.

Time is the Master *by John Holt plays.*

FRANKIE jumps up and looks at the door

POLICEMAN (OFF STAGE): Frankie—open up—it's the police.

They wait a few seconds and bang really loudly again.

POLICEMAN (OFF STAGE): Don't worry, Ken said you ave trouble getting up so we're here to help.

FRANKIE: I good.

POLICEMAN (OFF STAGE): We know. Our engines running and we ain't leaving without you—Five miles—every morning—rain or shine—with us beside yer. You can't win Ken his medal from bed now can yer? You coming out or we coming in?

KEN is in the office saying Hello and nodding and putting the phone down—picking it up and dialing. Doing the same action again and again.

54-46 by Toots and the Maytals plays.

The projector reads 1974.

GENE: Between the cake sales, bric a brac, raffle tickets, church events and donations including a big one from William Hill—we did it.

The day of the opening ceremony, me, Michael, my Mummy, his Mummy and his sisters and half the church all watched the telly to see Frankie carrying the St. Vincent flag with Ray beside him. The pair of them standing proud between Papua New Guinea and Sierra Leone.

The Show Must Go On *by Three Dog Night plays.*

At first FRANKIE is wearing a jacket and carrying a flag then the bell rings again and he takes off the jacket and starts to fight.

Then the bell rings again and he puts on another jacket to attend a meeting and nods politely to everyone.

Then the bell rings again and he's back fighting—it's almost slapstick in style.

GENE (CONTD): Trouble was, as Frankie and Ray were the entire St. Vincent team, besides being boxer and trainer, they had to be the flag bearers, Team Manager, Captain of the team, the officials required at all the official events AND wear all the different jackets.

KEN is on the phone in the office.

KEN: You arrived safe, Frankie?

(Beat.)

KEN (CONTD): Good. You make sure you call me after every fight, you hear? I want to know everything.

FRANKIE: I'll only call when I knock Inglan' out.

KEN: You do that, Frankie. Medal or no medal it will be a sweet victory.

FRANKIE: How you mean? I'm the odds-on favourite and I know you placed your bet weeks ago.

KEN: (*chuckles*) You know I did.

The bell rings once.

FRANKIE holds up his arms.

Crowds cheer. Music plays. FRANKIE dances.

FRANKIE: Hey, Gene? Me knock ENGLAND out.

GENE: How you feeling?

FRANKIE: Fantastic! Fan-bloody tastic!

GENE: So do I, Frankie, so do I.

FRANKIE puts down the phone.

The phone rings.

FRANKIE: Ken, you hear I won?

KEN: Course I did. What a day.

FRANKIE smiles and does a little shuffle.

FRANKIE: Just to warn you, they're saying I snubbed Princess Anne.

KEN: You did what to Princess Anne?

FRANKIE: Snubbed her.

KEN: Phew.

FRANKIE: (*Oblivious*) I was hungry as hell so I just popped into that event to show my face, not see anyone else's.

KEN: Ahh, that's not important, you're there to win medals not friends. Keep your eye on the prize, Frankie, nothing else. You ready for the final?

FRANKIE: If !!

The bell rings once.

FRANKIE climbs into the ring for the final.

Live commentary from Des Lynam plays as he fights… and at the end, a video plays archive footage of the final shot: The Zambian falling to the floor and FRANKIE smiling to the camera.

GENE: Look there. See that smile. It's all for me. My man from St. Vincent dropped by the England team not only wins gold but goes on to rob the entire England team of first position on the medal table by his one gold medal. Too sweet, too flipping sweet.

We hear a plane.

KEN is standing outside the ring in his police uniform.

FRANKIE walks onto stage and up to Ken. They hug and smile.

KEN: Welcome home, Frankie, welcome home. Was the England team on your flight?

FRANKIE: I dunno.

KEN: An Official from their welcoming party stood right next to where you are now and had the bloody cheek to tell me "Your guy struck lucky out there, Ken."

FRANKIE: And what you tell 'im?

KEN: To be careful. I'm in uniform, so clobbering him and arresting him in front of the press would be easy.

They both laugh.

You should have seen his face.

FRANKIE: I went for gold.

KEN: Ay and gold you got.I never doubted it, not for one second. Well done. You know it's time now—to go pro. We've gone as far as we can.

FRANKIE: I going all the way.

KEN: Dead right. I've set you up with George Francis. He's got Bunny Sterling and John Conteh European and World Champions. Both coloured.

FRANKIE: I know who he is but we parting like this, here?

KEN: We've spoke about that. I can't interfere with you and George. Anyway, you'll be busy training in North London and I'll be South inundated with kids wanting to join the club.

FRANKIE: Off the back of my win.

KEN: OUR win, and always the plan, dear Frankie. There's nothing else we can do for each other.

FRANKIE: Is that right? Here take this.

FRANKIE hands KEN his medal.

KEN: No I couldn't

FRANKIE: Claim your spoils. You worked as hard as me to get it.

KEN holds the medal to his chest.

KEN: This means a lot to me.

FRANKIE: It seem so. No stress, I gotta bigga fish to fry.

FRANKIE looks at him.

YOUNG VOICE (V/O): Daddy.

FRANKIE walks off towards it.

GENE: Happy Endings. Or were they? The club was busier than Piccadilly Circus, but with Ken so high up them police ranks Ray and Bruce Baker running it. St. Vincent invited Frankie back to a hero's welcome, seeing how they never won a gold medal before and only one more since and me and Michael, proud as punch, went with him. Going home, for me, felt like being held in Mummy's arms, but somehow Frankie felt lost, like his home soil couldn't feed his roots because, even if England poisoned his flower, it held his passion. So Frankie being the fighter that he is, came back carrying his unfulfilled promise in his suitcase to the cold of the UK, a basement flat, and a gym in Chalk Farm.

FADE TO BLACK.

ACT TWO

SCENE 1

October '74 comes up on a projector.

Lights move to the ring. A small man with grey wavy hair is standing in the centre of the ring sweeping the floor.

MFSB TSPO is playing. Loud.

On the projector a sign reads "a man who mistakes kindness for weakness is the weakest kind of man."

> *FRANKIE stands outside the ring. The man Looks over to FRANKIE, puts the broom to one side and looks at him. There is a moment's silence while both of them look at each other. Then FRANKIE looks around the gym.*

FRANKIE: Morning, Sir.

GEORGE: Call me George. Everyone else does

FRANKIE: Or Sargaent Major?

GEORGE: George is my name. Only John... John Conteh can call me that. Even if it's true. (*He winks*) Welcome to the home of champions.

> *FRANKIE doesn't move.*

What you waiting on?

FRANKIE: The magic.

GEORGE: Well com'on, soppy bullocks, get in.

> *He holds the rope up.*

The magic happens in 'ere at the four corners of truth.

> *FRANKIE climbs into the ring and stands in the centre looking at the four corners.*

GEORGE moves to one corner and stands by a stool.

FRANKIE moves to the next corner and sits on the stool.

FRANKIE: This feels good, Sir, I mean, George.

GEORGE: Ken said you were very polite.

FRANKIE: Good manners, bad behaviour.

GEORGE: Is that right?

FRANKIE: Me Mummy say so.

GEORGE: That's John Conteh's stool. You'll have to move.

There is silence as they both look at each other.

FRANKIE stays seated.

GEORGE: You deaf?

FRANKIE: No. Just comfortable.

GEORGE walks into the ring centre. They are watching each other.

GEORGE stands firm for a second and then motions FRANKIE to join him. FRANKIE slowly gets up and comes over. GEORGE walks around FRANKIE looking him up and down.

GEORGE: You like training, Frankie?

FRANKIE: IF? It's the best part of boxing.

GEORGE: Good, coz it's my religion. 5:30am every morning, rain or shine, a ten mile run over the heath, followed by a swim in the pond, topped off with breakfast at the cafe, before grabbing a kip and coming back for sparring, strength and conditioning work. Reckon you can handle that?

FRANKIE: I ready like steady.

GEORGE: Good. Coz you'll need to be in tip-top condition to win a few fights and grab Mickey Duff's attention. You know who he is, right?

FRANKIE: They call him MD cause he runs tings.

GEORGE: Like Smithfield's... but if we scratch his back maybe he'll align the stars and we'll touch the moon.

GEORGE winks.

FRANKIE gives a nervous smile.

GEORGE steps in front of him and places his hand on FRANKIE's chest

GEORGE: Your heart, Frankie, is your drive and will—

GEORGE holds FRANKIE's fist in his hand.

—Your punch is your inner and outer strength—

GEORGE holds FRANKIE's chin in his palm.

—and your chin your resilience

GEORGE nods and FRANKIE stops.

FRANKIE: And we swimming in them cold water ponds even in winter?

FRANKIE walks and sits on the stool in the next corner.

GEORGE: Especially in winter... But I do everything I ask you to do so you'll do everything I say with no questions. And, by the way, that's Bunny Sterling's spot. Sterling by name and Sterling by nature.

FRANKIE: I ain't next in line?

GEORGE: No. Not yet. In this stable we understand each corner represents a journey, roads travelled—and each seat paths crossed. You have to know a man and beat a man before you can take his seat, and deal with the victory and disappointment the same.

FRANKIE stands up and looks at GEORGE and then the two remaining corners.

FRANKIE: Disappointment just intent with no discipline.

GEORGE: And discipline is just learning to love the things you 'ate.

GEORGE points to a third corner.

GEORGE: Your place is there, Frankie.

FRANKIE: And you? Where's your place?

GEORGE: Mine? Wherever the fuck I want (*he winks*).

GEORGE leaves the ring. He turns the music up.

TSOP MFSB from 3.00 where Three Degrees sing "Let's get it on, time to get down" plays.

GEORGE: Well, what you waiting for?

FRANKIE: We train to music?

GEORGE: Always. Come on let's get you ready. Your debut fight's coming up.

FADE TO BLACK.

SCENE 2

A poster on the projector reads: 16th October 1974—Frankie Lucas vs Pat Brogan—Hilton Hotel, Mayfair, London.

The bell rings once.

FRANKIE goes to the centre of the ring.

GEORGE: It's time for the good, the bad and the ugly. Go'on, Frankie, get out there and take no hostages. Nice and easy, stay relaxed, keep him moving.
Ah really good, Frankie, try that right hook to the body.
That's it, lovely, very nice, cool calm, try your left hook.

FRANKIE doesn't do it.

LEFT HOOK

GEORGE is forceful but FRANKIE carries on not listening. We hear the sound of punches being taken.

GEORGE: *(Shouting)* THE LEFT FUCKING HOOK!

FRANKIE moves in more aggressively and lands a left hook—we hear a body fall. GEORGE rushes into the middle of the ring and hugs FRANKIE.

GEORGE: A round one knockout on your first fight. You happy with that?

FRANKIE: Over the moon. I fought as me spirit tell me, George, no disrespect.

They walk back to the corner. The crowd is still noisy but moved back to chatter.

GEORGE: You won didn't yer? 'Ave a look? Front row third seat. You've made MD smile.

GEORGE winks at FRANKIE.

Bunny's turn now. Another pearl to my string. You staying?

FRANKIE: Yeah, man! We a winning family.

GEORGE picks up the towels and the bag and they both leave the ring.

Band on the Run *plays and the projector shows the photo of George, John and Bunny naked.*

GENE: Family? Suddenly South London became real far from North. Frankie was so excited being part of the 'who wants them brigade' George was so proud of, he forget where to place his feet. It felt like every two minutes George and one of his boxers were in court tearing up the rule book and putting photos of their backsides in the papers to boot. I tried to tell Frankie that trouble don' set up like rain but, for the first time, Frankie felt like he was part of something, of the change being made. So the only thing holding us, he, me and Michael together, was the phone box on the corner and the 68 bus.

FADE TO BLACK.

SCENE 3

Lights come up on GEORGE.

The Projector shows a photo of George Francis, Bunny Johnson and John Conteh naked.

GEORGE enters the stage fuming.

GEORGE: Oi, you lot. I know yer 'ere.

We hear giggles in the dark. Then the lights come up.

FRANKIE: Wot appen? You ain't feel to swim today?

GEORGE: I was gonna till some fella said I won the case, but lost me boxers

Giggles again.

Very bloody funny. Well, as none of you did the swim I'll be fucked if I'm paying for breakfast.

FRANKIE: John said that was our Christmas brunch.

GEORGE: (*Smiling*) You know he's always wanted to do a runner from the bill. You're lucky it's Christmas otherwise I'd sack the lot of yer.

GEORGE gets a bottle of whiskey out of his desk drawer and two glasses. He pours drinks.

FRANKIE: And lose a stable of champions?

FRANKIE picks up his glass and knocks it with GEORGE's.

GEORGE: The who wants them brigade?

FRANKIE: You. You want us.

GEORGE: I do. And you're part of this band of brothers

FRANKIE: Yeah, man, I found my place.

GEORGE nods.

FRANKIE (CONTD): I can roll a smoke?

GEORGE gets up and goes and plays Matt Munro Impossible Dream.

GEORGE: Ain't that illegal? *(Smiles).*

FRANKIE: You getting merry for Christmas?

GEORGE: Yeah, watching Morecambe and Wise and eating too much. You?

FRANKIE: Partying and eating black cake.

GEORGE: Like our Dundee cake?

FRANKIE: No. Dundee cake lighter. We soak our fruits in rum.

GEORGE: We soak ours in whiskey.

FRANKIE: But not from October, so watch what you say.

GEORGE: I've been to Jamaica. I know food in Jamaica is a matter of state. *(Laughs).*

FRANKIE: You been to Jamaica?

GEORGE: Yeah with Bunny. After we broke the ten-year rule, the bastards sent us halfway round the world to defend his title.

FRANKIE: Did he win?

GEORGE: Drew. We went from Australia to Jamaica but Bunny loved it, fighting to his home crowd as a Champion, and the bender after.

FRANKIE: Jamaican sorrel?

GEORGE: Fucking lethal. I thought, portering in Covent Garden, I knew every fruit known to man but sorrel and breadfruit were new to me.

FRANKIE: Like the cold and paraffin heaters to me when I reach here. Does Joan make your Christmas Cake?

GEORGE: Leave off. The bakery up Pratt Street does ours.

FRANKIE: Where?

GEORGE: Top end of Camden Town. I'm a very loyal customer seeing how the baker there got me into boxing.

FRANKIE: How so?

GEORGE: He trained at St. Pancras and took a shine to me. Me ol' man was a bit of a boat and proper handy, and I was a skinny and scrawny kid, looking after the rag n bones man's horses next door. So I guess he must have thought I needed a little help and took me. The rest, as they say, is history.

FRANKIE: How old was you?

GEORGE: 11.

FRANKIE: I was nine. Were you any good?

GEORGE: Nah, I was too much of a brawler to earn prize money but I loved it, the training, the smell of the sawdust and sweat, the noise. But most of all I loved the training—it made me feel free, know what I mean?

FRANKIE: Yeah, man.

GEORGE: Then one day Bunny came in with Lennie Gibbs and I saw him fight. His gentle manner, his skill in the ring, his timing, the way he used his brain as well as his body, the art of his boxing, I knew then training was my bag, and I had to work him. So I went out on a limb, left the portering and St. Pancras and went pro as a manager.

FRANKIE: He wasn't better than John?

GEORGE: Different.

FRANKIE: Not better than me.

GEORGE: That remains to be seen. Bunny's greatness is in his precision and his dedication to the sport. He could have been anything he wanted but he chose to graft as a kitchen porter to keep himself wedded to the ring. My Mrs said if he can do it so can we and supported me and the kids until we got going.

FRANKIE: My Gene's been doing all the heavy lifting for three years now.

GEORGE: You wanna thank your lucky stars you've got her.

FRANKIE: I do but I can't keep going home empty-handed.

GEORGE: No one said this game is easy.

FRANKIE: But as hard as it is to find a pound note, I don't see myself as a kitchen porter.

GEORGE: What? You wanna stay focused on the work and let the rest follow.

FRANKIE: Money has no patience and time waits on no man. So how long before I get a shot at Minter?

GEORGE: That's down to your commitment to the work. My future depends mainly on myself. The great Paul Robeson said that. See that sign?

He points to the kindness sign on the wall.

It reminds me knowing the pain of poverty helps weather the pain of progress. We're making change here Frankie with World, European and British champions and that's bigger than what you can't or won't do and one fight.

FRANKIE: I can't make change with no blasted matches?

GEORGE: What's for you won't pass you. And I only deal in talent.

FRANKIE pushes his glass forward and takes his spliff from behind his ear.

FRANKIE doesn't light the spliff but carries on holding it and goes to put it in his mouth.

GEORGE: Look we've both got homes to go to

FRANKIE puts the spliff away like a kid

Ere' take this score from me get your littl'un something nice for Christmas and, next year, I'll pay yer to spar with John and Bunny. How does that sound?

FRANKIE takes the money

FRANKIE: Boom Boom Minter and a title sounds better.

They both grin.

GEORGE: Go on, get outta here, go home to your wife and kid, coz remember, at the end of the day your boy and your missus is all you really got.

FRANKIE: Merry Christmas, George.

GEORGE: Merry Christmas, Frankie.

FRANKIE leaves the office and walks towards the sofa where GENE is sitting.

FRANKIE: Get ready, gal. Dress Michael nice. We going to fete by Marcia and Franklin. 1975 gonna be our year. The year I rob Minter or tek a title me nah care which and when I do...

GENE: ...The world gonna see the man I see.
(*And then she speaks to the audience*) So, like a fool, I make myself look sweeter than the sorrell, to sit at the bottom of the stairs, watching night turn to day, waiting for that damn doorbell to ring.

FADE TO BLACK.

SCENE 4

Pomp and Pride *by Toots and the Maytals plays.*

FRANKIE enters the gym

GEORGE is in the office reading the Boxing News and sports papers.

GEORGE: Good Christmas?

FRANKIE: Lovely thanks. Whatcha' doin'?

GEORGE: Sorting out your title chasers. John's defending his title.

FRANKIE: What the papers saying?

GEORGE: They're calling me a "white witch doctor."

FRANKIE: (*Laughs*) And me a "white-hating savage."

GEORGE: Well, I suppose what don't kill yer makes yer stronger.

GEORGE throws the papers in the bin

FRANKIE: Constant drips seep in slow.

(Beat.)

How come John don't get the same hate?

GEORGE: He bought a world title back to these shores after 22 years. What's not to love?

FRANKIE: And he born 'ere.

GEORGE: Born here or not. He's pound for pound the best athlete I've ever trained. With as much charisma.

FRANKIE: An English Mohammed Ali.

GEORGE: (*Laughs*) Well as it 'appens John did ask his advice.

FRANKIE: For what?

GEORGE: For winning. We were in Paris. John and him had this proper banter going. We were at the Arc de Triomphe when Ali winked at John and said "watch this." Like a bloody messiah he strolled into the middle of the traffic and just stood there. In a blink of an eye, he caused a road block, cars stalled with people clambering to get his autograph, he signed a few, looked back at us, laughed, and started to trott away before turning round looking at John and shouting: "fight as a light heavyweight."

FRANKIE: And he took the advice?

GEORGE: Dead right. Ali has people power, John's getting it and you'll find it. Win that world title, Frankie, and for five minutes, the press and everyone else, will love you...

(Beat.)

...more than afternoon tea at the Ritz.

FRANKIE: You want I spar with John?

GEORGE: Yeah, but take it easy.

FRANKIE: Why? You scared I'm gonna hurt his brittle hands?

GEORGE: Wot like Minter's eye?

They both giggle.

Joking aside, I know you know better.

Kung Fu Fighting *by Carl Douglas plays.*

We stay on GEORGE in his corner. He is deep in thought. We hear punches landing and a yelp.

What's happening?

FRANKIE: John hurt his hands on my hard head.

GEORGE: *(Irritated)* For fuck's sake, Frankie. You deaf? Nothing's never easy with you.

FRANKIE: No, George, nothing's ever easy FOR me.

FRANKIE smirks.

GEORGE: Ha bloody ha. Well, when you're at Wembley make it count, feel the crowd, soak up the atmosphere, 'cause John will win and win big.

FRANKIE: I going to Wembley?

GEORGE: Oh, did I forget to tell yer? You're on John's undercard.

The projector shows a poster for 3rd March 1975 Wembly Arena. John Conteh vs Lonnie Bennett World Light Heavyweight Title.

Fight—Frankie Lucas vs Joe Gregory.

Lights go down

We hear loud cheers and applause with chants of 'Conteh' and a commentator declaring John Conteh World Champion.

FRANKIE dances and calls over to GENE.

FRANKIE: Gene? You ain't hear? Me and John both win.

GENE: Congratulations. I guess the champagne's flowing.

FRANKIE: Sure is and right now I'm full o' beans.

GENE: Good coz we missing the steak and egg.

FRANKIE: Good ting we nah fill we bellies so then.

GENE: Huh. You passing by?

FRANKIE: I busy with a world champion.

GENE: Busy with one don't make you one.

(Beat.)

We ain't seen you since Christmas

FRANKIE: You need anything?

GENE: A whole heap of everything. And don't tell me to pass by your mother's house. I feel like I marry to she.

FRANKIE: Michael want something?

GENE: *(She pauses to think)* A tricycle. At nursery he's always on a little blue tricycle.

(Beat.)

FRANKIE: And you?

GENE: Space. Enough space for us.

FRANKIE: When I win the world title, Gene, I tekin' us back a yard, straight to your mummy's arms.

Lights go down.

SCENE 5

Pressure Drop by Toots *and the Maytals plays.*

GEORGE in the ring—sitting on a corner stool and then moving to another corner stool.

FRANKIE marches in agitated and forceful.

FRANKIE: Oi, George. You sort out any moves for us title chasers?

GEORGE: As it happens I have. But you won't like it. I'm working Bunny for the British title.

FRANKIE: What about me?

GEORGE: You're not a contender.

FRANKIE: How ya mean?

GEORGE: Because, unless I'm mistaken, you don't hold the Southern Area title.

GEORGE gets out of the ring and walks to his office.

FRANKIE follows him—talking to GEORGE's back.

FRANKIE: (*Speaking to himself*) I ain't a contender?

GEORGE: Bunny's a better one who draws a bigger crowd.

FRANKIE: So I need crowds to get fights and fights to get crowds

GEORGE stops at his desk and turns round to face FRANKIE.

GEORGE: Yeah, you do. Don't you know MD says "all black boxers bring to the ring is their bags"?

FRANKIE: And now you sprouting the same shit? Ferocious Frankie bring nuff people. Whose he fighting anyway?

GEORGE sits down at his desk.

GEORGE: Maurice Hope.

FRANKIE: He ain't even a middleweight and he's black.

GEORGE: Imagine that, two black West Indian boxers.

FRANKIE: British citizens.

GEORGE: Fighting for the British title. If you don't mind I'm busy.

FRANKIE: I do mind.

GEORGE: Tough. I promised Bunny a world title.

FRANKIE: A promise is a comfort to a fool.

GEORGE: Show some respect, you tosser. If it weren't for me and Bunny you'd still be waiting 10 years for a title shot.

FRANKIE: (*He imitates GEORGE*) "I know. 30 years ago, Britain had a colour ban followed by the 10 year rule and all the cartels."

GEORGE: (*With real surpressed anger*) You taking the piss?... Me and Bunny fucking paid for you

FRANKIE: You paid for me to wait my turn?

GEORGE: (*Anger building*) You cheeky Bastard. Bunny fought like poetry in motion to get that title, but it was like we'd nicked the trophy out of the cupboard with the near lynching we got.

FRANKIE: We?

GEORGE: Yeah, we. The hate mail I got through my door, my local boozer refusing to serve me.

FRANKIE: Boxing never neutral.

GEORGE: (*In temper*) I know. We had a fight at the RAF hangers, We won hands down but didn't get the decision.

FRANKIE: So he wasn't a happy Bunny then?

GEORGE: No he wasn't, as we stormed out, MD kicked over a bucket of whitewash right by Bunny's feet. "You'll need that if you wanna win fights round here my son," he said.

FRANKIE: Landing different to arriving.

GEORGE: First thing Bunny did when he bagged the British title was square up to MD, straight in the eyes he said, "I beat your ticketseller, fair and square, and I didn't need no whitewash to do it." I knew then he kissed the world title shot goodbye.

(*Beat.*)

He's owed another shot.

FRANKIE: So I'm on ice for Bunny's dues?

GEORGE: No, you're on ice 'cause you party harder than you train.

FRANKIE: It's not my debt, George, I've had one fight all year.

GEORGE: I owe him.

FRANKIE: What! You marry to he?

GEORGE: No. You're just not in the mix.

FRANKIE: You know you 'ave more than one boxer?

FRANKIE leaves the office but as he reaches the ring he turns and goes back in GEORGE looks up and preempts him.

GEORGE: I know. I've got a responsibility to all my boxers, and a plan for you too.

FRANKIE: It don't feel so.

GEORGE: Win the Southern Area title, Bunny will vacate the British for the European, then you can jump in against Finneghan or Minter.

He hangs on Minter knowing FRANKIE will respond to it.

FRANKIE: Minter?

GEORGE: Why do you want him so bad?

FRANKIE: Him people got no behaviour. You hurt one, you hurt them all.

GEORGE: So get busy moving or get busy losing.

FRANKIE: Set the match but after JUST don't tell me to wait.

(Beat.)

GEORGE: Stop waging wars. Choose your battles wisely.

FRANKIE: If push ever come to shove, and I have to fight Bunny, will you know your corner?

GEORGE: I'm not your enemy, Frankie, so do yourself a favour. Go home.

FADE TO BLACK.

SCENE 6

Boxing Around by Cornell Campbell plays as the lights go down.

FRANKIE starts to mumble and is getting paranoid. He sits on his sofa and shouts to GENE. GENE is on the office side of the stage.

FRANKIE: Gene?

GENE: Frankie?

FRANKIE: Who else calling you?

GENE: I'm just leaving for night classes.

FRANKIE: What you doing at night classes?

GENE: A secretarial course. Michael is at your mother's house if you feel to look for he.

FRANKIE: Bunny getting the title shot.

GENE: Ohh, that must hurt. You OK? You want to come round later?

FRANKIE: I can't tonight.

GENE: Why your yard full'o' feet?

FRANKIE: No, I got stuff doing.

GENE: Is it really? Well, I don't see no ring on me or you in the ring.

FRANKIE: I working my chances, Gene. The rings soon come.

GENE: I hope so because I can't live in the shadow of your choices and chances forever.

The projector shows a poster. The Southern Area Title, October 27th 1975. Frankie Lucas vs Jan Magdziarz, National Sporting Club, Cafe Royale, London.

FRANKIE is sitting in the corner and GEORGE is behind him, rubbing his shoulders.

GEORGE: Take it easy, Frankie. Keep him moving, keep him working, protect your chin, go for the body, save your left hook, cunning like a fox. Don't brawl, box. Control wins a fight.

FRANKIE gets up and goes into the middle.

Bell rings

RING ANNOUNCER: Round one.

GEORGE: That's it.

There is the sound of clashing heads from the ring.

GENE looks at the ring

GENE: Frankie wanted me there. He reckoned the weed make him strong but I fire up his will. So I went, but his rage was so strong, he didn't even throw me a smile. The two of them charged and locked heads like stags mating. Blood streaming everywhere. And even though Frankie's head is as hard as his ears, his eye soft.

Bell rings once.

FRANKIE and GEORGE are in the corner GEORGE is tending to Frankie.

GEORGE: Four neat, tight stitches. Better than a Saville Row tailor. Now get back out there. And wallop him around the ring.

Bell rings.

RING ANNOUNCER: Round two.

FRANKIE goes back to the middle.

GEORGE: YES!

The fight is stopped

Bell rings.

RING ANNOUNCER: And the winner is Frankie Lucas.

FRANKIE comes back to the corner. The audience are booing and it is targeted at FRANKIE.

FRANKIE: (*Smiling*) Happy with that?

GEORGE: (*Pats his back*) Very.

FRANKIE: One down, one to go.

GEORGE: That your girl out there?

FRANKIE looks to GENE.

Go home, let yer boy know you've won. Enjoy the win.

GENE: He enjoyed his win alright. Sending me home in a cab as stitched up as his eye.

FADE TO BLACK

SCENE 7

Chant Down Babylon by Bob Marley plays.

FRANKIE is on the sofa getting ready to watch the projector. MICHAEL is next to him. There is a small stool beside them. The projector shows a poster: 4th November 1975, Alan Minter vs Kevin Finnegan for the British Title. Empire Pool. Wembley

We hear the commentary play.

FRANKIE: Com'on Michael' come watch this. You hear them vultures? Picking my bones. Bunny vacated for me, not them, not to fight each other. You see how these people rob me so easy?

MICHAEL moves away.

FRANKIE: Where you going? Here, come hold some chocolate

The projector shows the last round. It is a ferocious fight and Minter is winning as the crowd erupts. FRANKIE gets up, paces up and down, kicks his stool over and starts punching the wall.

FRANKIE: Michael, you getting tall whilst me money getting short. Another Christmas comin' with me empty hands holding.

MICHAEL cries / whimpers.

Why you cry?

Yo nah know cry cry baby ain't get nah rights.

The kid takes deep breaths as he sighs. FRANKIE calms down a little and picks up the chocolate and the crisps.

Look take some crisps?

FRANKIE paces and then sits down.

Hold still with me, your Mummy soon come to tek yeh.

FRANKIE moves with shame and holds out his hand.

Tek me hand.

Yer don't wanna tek me hand, Michael?

I smell to you?

We hear a key in the door and the door close.

GENE comes in and looks perturbed. She takes off her coat and holds it over her arms feeling the atmosphere.

GENE: What happened, Frankie?

FRANKIE: We watching boxing.

GENE: Why's he crying so?

FRANKIE: Man, the cries do come to he too easy, you too soft on he.

GENE: You punching the wall, Frankie?

FRANKIE: I stopping the duppy.

GENE: *(With trepidation in her voice)* You stopping the duppy?

GENE starts to slowly put her coat back on and motions to MICHAEL to join her.

FRANKIE: *(Realising the trepidation in her voice back tracks)* I imagin' Minter's head.

GENE: You ain't late for the gym?

GENE starts to walk backwards towards the door slowly.

Come, Michael, let's we go and leave Daddy in peace.

We hear the door slam shut.

FRANKIE is alone on the sofa looking confused.

FADE TO BLACK.

SCENE 8

The projector shows a poster: Alan Minter vs Frankie Lucas. The Royal Albert Hall.

GEORGE is in the ring he is sweeping, arranging the stools, dancing a little to The Marvelettes' The Hunter Gets Captured by the Game.

FRANKIE comes in looking sharp.

GEORGE: Oh, look what the cat dragged in? Nice and early and looking lively. You 'ad a rest?

FRANKIE: Yeah. This champion ready to be tested. I was beginning to give up on you, George.

GEORGE: Boxers never like to give up, Frankie.

FRANKIE: But my time has come, it's me now.

GEORGE: Well, don't hang about, go on, get changed.

The phone rings.

GEORGE leaves the ring to go answear it.

GEORGE: (*After a pause*) Hello? No I don't need to sit... What do you mean trouble in paradise? Minter don't wanna fight him. He wants to fight Trevor Francis!! The Welterweight? You're not serious... Defend his Southern Area title?... No, I won't calm down. He won that last fight fair and square... I won't regret it.

GEORGE bangs the phone down and throws his broom across the stage.

FRANKIE walks in he sees GEORGE in a temper and unable to look him in the eye.

GEORGE: (*He shouts*) Frankie, we're going out.

FRANKIE: If you've got something bad to tell me. Don't.

FRANKIE turns around and walks out.

They will Rob You by John Holt plays.

GENE: It was in the bleak mid-winter of January when Minter defended his title against Trevor Francis. But Frankie had to wait until the budding springs of March before defending his Southern Area title, against the same fella he won it off. Frankie asked me to fire his will again but, to be truthful, I was glad north so far from south because that Duppy business stole the twinkle in my eye.
The rematch happened at the Grosvenor House hotel. They both locked heads again and the blood streamed again but this time Frankie's blood flowed like the river to the sea.

I don't know if Frankie just lacked the double hunger needed to win or the other guy just had more to prove.

GEORGE and FRANKIE are back in the corner of the ring.

GEORGE is behind FRANKIE.

FRANKIE is sitting looking dazed whilst GEORGE tends to his eye.

FRANKIE: George, you're real good at tending to damage.

GEORGE: Not this. I can't fix this.

FRANKIE puts his hand up to blood streaming down his face.

FRANKIE: But you good at fixing things. I feel the devil strong in this hand. It pretty like a piano player's hand. Playing my power and my fate.

GEORGE: You alright, Frankie?

FRANKIE: No, George, I'm hurt.

GEORGE walks away.

Lonely Soldier by Gregory Issacs plays.

GENE: He didn't get another fight till December and then he got disqualified. George blamed the weed but with just seven matches in two years, all that training had Frankie like a pent-up lion in a cage.

GENE looks at her hand. She flashes an engagement ring.

GENE (CONTD): And I had a new beau in tow because with Michael coming on for five and ready for school, and with no purses, Frankie could barely feed Ital him cat. I mean it stands to reason a gal con't live on bread alone.

FADE TO BLACK.

SCENE 9

Lights come up on GEORGE in his office and FRANKIE walking straight in with proper attitude.

FRANKIE: You can handle a spar with me, George?

GEORGE: Yeah. I'll try not to hurt yer.

FRANKIE: You sure?

They walk towards the ring—GEORGE after FRANKIE.

GEORGE: I'll try my hardest.

They get in the ring.

FRANKIE: Where's my shot? I waited and watched. John's 'ad his. Bunny got his and both of them gone.

He shuffles by GEORGE.

Minter and Finnegan got theirs.

FRANKIE whacks GEORGE hard.

GEORGE: And you'll get yours, Frankie.

GEORGE punches FRANKIE's head.

FRANKIE punches GEORGE low.

FRANKIE: I had two fights all year and none of them named Minter or carry a title.

GEORGE: YOU lost the regional, Frankie, no one else.

GEORGE gives him a punch to the belly

But don't worry the fat lady ain't sung yet.

FRANKIE: Where she singing? The wailing wall?

FRANKIE punches GEORGE in the gut—GEORGE reels back.

Black boxers can't always be the gifts that keep on giving.

GEORGE: Giving what?

GEORGE punches FRANKIE in the gut.

FRANKIE reels back and comes forward.

FRANKIE: Fuck you and this fucking waiting game. When's my time?

FRANKIE does a flurry of quick punches to the body.

GEORGE steps back and misses the last blow.

GEORGE: You're a guaranteed hard fight, Frankie.

FRANKIE: How yer mean?

FRANKIE moves forward and catches GEORGE with a left hook.

You saying only the Devil wanna battle me?

GEORGE: Must you carry the Devil's rage alright, but it's the smoking making you paranoid.

He punches GEORGE round the head hard.

FRANKIE: You think because my eye bad I can't see the truth? That I wait and watch as everyone moves on. Whilst all my roads lead to a stonewall.

GEORGE: (*Reels back*) The truth is in the commitment to the work.

FRANKIE: I still 'ere doing. What's all this for, George?

GEORGE: Tomorrow, Frankie. It's all our struggle.

FRANKIE: Don't mix up my head. Ken say you owe me money.

FRANKIE comes off the ropes and pushes GEORGE into the corner.

GEORGE: What?

GEORGE sidesteps FRANKIE but FRANKIE corners GEORGE with immense intimidation.

FRANKIE: My spirit vexed. All this strength with no power is a fucking waste of time and my clock ticking.

FRANKIE pushes GEORGE hard against the corner pole.

GEORGE: Look, the game's the game. We got no choice but to play it.

GEORGE swings a jab at FRANKIE who falls back against the ropes to miss it and then FRANKIE grabs GEORGE by the throat.

FRANKIE: Just get me some fights or pay me some money.

FRANKIE suddenly realises what he isdoing and lets GEORGE go.

FRANKIE storms off but without direction.

Gene Gene Gene—where are you?

GENE (O/S): I busy, Frankie.

FRANKIE: Gene? Is that you?

GENE (O/S): Yes, Frankie. You OK?

There is a silence.

Back a Yard *by The Abyssians plays.*

FRANKIE: Gene, you remember Christmas back home? How it start with the smell of rum in October and how by December the cherries mek the air drip with the seasons sweet scent?

GENE (O/S): Along with the sorrell and the cleaning that signal Christmas startin'.

FRANKIE: And in the yard we be fattenin' up one special white fowl that we catch to kill and cook.

GENE (O/S): To compliment the pork.

FRANKIE: And then we go to nine mornings.

GENE comes on stage and walks over to him.

FRANKIE puts his arm around GENE's waist. The two of them dance and sway, remembering better times.

To see the bright lights, feel the joy. Like just being together the reason for the season.

FRANKIE stops dancing and stares.

FRANKIE: What was I saying?

GENE moves away.

FRANKIE stands looking at her.

GENE: I busy, Frankie, I have to go.

GENE walks off stage with her back to him.

FRANKIE: But I wanna come home, Gene, I wanna see you.

GENE stops and turns to look at him

GENE: You can't. I carrying child, Frankie. And you don't wanna see that.

GENE walks off quickly,

FRANKIE is left alone on the stage, bewilded.

The lights go down.

INTERVAL

SCENE 10

The theme tune from Rocky, Gonna Fly Now, *by Bill Conti is on.*

GEORGE is sweeping the ring.

The projector reads: 1977.

GEORGE: New broom sweeps clean, Frankie. Your seat's ready.

FRANKIE: Where's Bunny?

GEORGE: Retired to be a carpet salesman. Boza-Edwards's got his seat. Clinton McKenzies is in John's. And you? You're good right?

FRANKIE: Where's John?

GEORGE: On a wander after his strike and all that funny business. We're in a new chapter.

FRANKIE: So, I'm centre stage?

GEORGE: You've got a fight in five weeks so let's get this show on the road

FRANKIE: That right?

GEORGE: Yeah. You ready to train like the clappers?

FRANKIE: I ready to prove them wrong.

GEORGE: Without the rage?

FRANKIE: My temper parked.

GEORGE: That's the spirit. Do that and the fights will come so fast your feet won't touch the ground.

FRANKIE: Are we all that remains, George?

GEORGE: Try to see your loss as a freedom, Frankie.

(Beat.)

FRANKIE: Say less. Do more.

FRANKIE goes to the centre of the ring and starts to spar.

The bell rings.

The projector flashes like flash cards. Fast and furious behind FRANKIE are posters of: 21st March 1977 Frankie vs Wayne Bennett, Cafe Royale, Piccadilly, London.

FRANKIE holds him arm up as a winner.

The bell rings twice.

The projector flashes a poster of: 12th April 1977 Frankie vs Alex Tompkins, Royal Albert Hall, Kensington London.

FRANKIE holds up his arm victorious but the sounds are really hostile because FRANKIE is undercard on Minter's bill.

The bell rings three times.

The projector shows a poster: 1977 31st May for the British Middleweight Title. Frankie Lucas vs Kevin Finnegan, Royal Albert Hall. This remains on the projector.

GENE: Look at that. Frankie had just nine fights in three long years to reach the billing on that poster. So much blood, sweat and tears written on the wall. He'd waited nigh on his whole life for that shot, well, that and Minter. But win or lose, with so much water under the bridge, there was no bringing back what had already gone.

The lights go down,

FRANKIE is in his corner, GEORGE is rubbing his shoulders.

FRANKIE: He is a bull but me is a lion and lion nam bull!

GEORGE: You got this. We're almost there. I can feel your strength. It's like a kettle on the boil. Just don't let it boil over. Stay on one round at a time. Go on.

The bell rings.

FRANKIE gets up and goes to the centre with strength in his stride.

We hear heads clashing.

Lights go down.

The projector shows archive footage from the fight. It goes straight to Round Ten.

GEORGE: No, Frankie, No!

The bell rings.

FRANKIE goes to the corner dazed but with conviction. GEORGE sits him down looking at his eye.

THE REFEREE (V/O): By TKO in Round 11 the winner is Kevin Finnegan.

FRANKIE: It's OK. Me can fight still.

GEORGE: The cut's too deep. It's over, Frankie.

FRANKIE: No, I can fight. Let me fight. Let me win.

GEORGE: (*Still tending to his eye*) You have won, all that praying at the ponds paid off. That was a fight for the history books, Frankie. You done me proud. You done yourself proud. Best I've seen yer.

FRANKIE: Finnegan wasn't the better man.

GEORGE: No. The only thing that stopped you is that bloody eyebrow. Hold your head up. Everyone's gonna wanna see the rematch.

FRANKIE holds his head up and looks in GEORGE's eyes.

FRANKIE: Fighting like the buses, you wait forever, then three come in a row. The waiting make you more tired than the walk.

Lights go down.

Here I Come *by Dennis Brown plays.*

FRANKIE is relaxing on his sofa, playing with his hand, punching the air and smoking a spliff.

The Radio announces Minter taking the British title back off Finnegan and the commentary states Minter has a big purse.

GEORGE in in the gym on the phone.

FRANKIE walks into the gym. GEORGE puts down the phone.

GEORGE: I was waiting for you. I've just fixed you a stint abroad.

FRANKIE: My business here.

GEORGE: It's quick cash.

FRANKIE: It's not about the money.

GEORGE: Blimey, you've changed your tune, which is a shame, because it's a big purse.

FRANKIE: Five figure big?

GEORGE: Don't be silly, Frankie.

FRANKIE: How much did Finnegan get for our fight, George? And Minter's fight?

GEORGE: I dunno.

FRANKIE: Was I like Bunny?

GEORGE: What?

FRANKIE: Bunny getting ten percent of what Finnegan got when Finnegan robbed his title. Was that the same for me?

GEORGE: And me getting twenty percent of his ten percent including the stoppages?

FRANKIE: So John Conteh went on strike to benefit Minter, not us?

GEORGE: Where's all this coming from? John went on strike because he said MD weren't acting in his best interest, so MD had him up in front of the board and John had no choice but to get up the Strand to sue him.

FRANKIE: And he won.

GEORGE: Yes. You know he won. I always made him right but no one really won, not in the end.

FRANKIE: But he got paid more?

GEORGE: Yes.

FRANKIE: That sound like winning to me.

GEORGE: MD lost the case. Boxers get paid more, granted, but I had to stop managing him and no one looked after his hands like me, and he couldn't claw back the time he lost. So, yeah, he earned more but he spent more—and on what?

FRANKIE: What ever the fuck he wanted, George. He just stopped taking the punches to stop you lot taking the pounds.

GEORGE: Careful, Frankie.

FRANKIE: Your name was on the contract so he sue you too.

GEORGE: I was caught between a rock and a hard place.

FRANKIE: Back home we say, de' tongue dat buy yo does sell yo.

GEORGE: And here we say don't bite the hand that feeds you. I walk a constant tightrope between Mickey's interests and my stable.

FRANKIE: A man can't have two masters, George.

GEORGE: I do right by all of you and no one can doubt that. Look, do you want this fucking trip abroad or not?

FRANKIE: Yeah.

(Beat.)

If I come back to a title match.

GEORGE: Well, right here, right now, we got three fights and three good paydays up for grabs.

FRANKIE: I'll take 'em because right here right now I'm the best shot you got.

GEORGE: (*Frustrated*) D'yer reckon?

(*Beat.*)

You play chess Frankie?

FRANKIE shakes his head.

I did't think so. Well, I do and it's a fucking hard game.

Lights go down and come back up again.

The Rocky Music plays again.

The projector shows two posters in quick succession:
1977-11-19 FRANKIE LUCAS vs ANGELO JACOPUCCI, Pala Ruffini, Torino.

FRANKIE does a small fight sequence and

RING ANNOUNCER: And the winner is Frankie Lucas.

PROJECTOR SHOWS SECOND POSTER
1978-01-07 Frankie Lucas Vs Norberto Rufino Cabrera, Palasport di San Siro, Milan.

FRANKIE does a small fight sequence..

RING ANNOUNCER: And the winner is Frankie Lucas.

The projector stays on the third poster: 22nd April 1978, FRANKIE LUCAS vs WILLIE 'The Worm' MONROE Teatro Ariston, San Remo Italy.

GEORGE: Right, listen, you've had two good fights back-to-back but Willie 'The Worm" Munroe IS tough. Very tough. It's gonna be hard. But you can do it if you keep your cool.

Lights go to darkness.

We hear jazz music.

A dance sequence shows a metaphorical fight—voices from the past, all the characters coming as FRANKIE falls down—it's a battle of his mind and he is losing.

REFEREE (V/O): By TKO in Round Eight—the winner is Willie "The Worm" Monroe.

FRANKIE is obviously shaken. He goes back to his corner to GEORGE.

FRANKIE: *(Tears welling in his eyes)* I had my guard up, George, trying to box using my head, but he was still catching me with those left hooks, savage left hooks, and I just kept taking the beating and I couldn't dig deep enough to give him anything back. Is that what all that waiting was for?

GEORGE: Your mind lost you that fight, Frankie, nothing else.

FRANKIE: All this struggle. What's the prize, George?

GEORGE: Winning, Frankie. And what we do with it.

The lights go down.

FRANKIE is on the sofa he calls over to GENE but there is no answer.

The lights come up.

FRANKIE is listening to the radio: Minter takes the European but his opponent dies in the ring. John loses to Pavlov.

FRANKIE starts to look at his hands, particularly the left hand. He looks about himself and in the mirror. He looks into the ring and shouts...

FRANKIE: These still the four corners of truth?

GEORGE: *(Shouts back)* You alright, Frankie?

FRANKIE: I feel for a rest, George.

GEORGE: Not yet, we still got work to do.

FRANKIE: Like?

GEORGE: A little exhibition tour in Zambia, courtesy of the African boxers in my stable.

FRANKIE: I think I'd like that, George.

GEORGE: You'll love it. And it's a four-figure pay day. They say a change is as good as a rest. Let's get out there

Lights go down and come up bright.

FRANKIE is centre stage running on the spot. He is running to cheers and people supporting him—like Ali in the Rumble in the Jungle documentary.

The projector shows a poster: 30th September 1978 Frankie Lucas vs Chiandro Mutti-Lusaka Zambia.

FRANKIE is in the centre of the ring and GEORGE raises his hand.

RING ANNOUNCER (V/O): And the winner by TKO is Frankie Lucas.

The cheers are mad. African chanting and support. FRANKIE loves it.

FRANKIE: I can finally get Michael 'im blue tricycle. So he can come. He don't come anymore.

GEORGE: What you talking about, Frankie?

FRANKIE: The journey too long.

GEORGE: He'll be back. You'll be back. Win the title and things will look different.

FRANKIE: Your mouth to God's ears. Wait, what title?

GEORGE: I've got you the re-match with Finnegan for the British Title.

FRANKIE: Finnegan? Where's Minter?

GEORGE: In Las Vegas on a six-figure purse. Bag the title Frankie and we'll be over there too, on our big payday. I reckon our chickens could be coming home to roost.

Lights go down.

The projector reads: April 10th 1979 Frankie Lucas vs Tony Sibson, Royal Albert Hall, London.

We hear boos and hostilities echo.

FRANKIE and GEORGE are in the ring warming up.

GEORGE: I know Finnegan pulled out but don't underestimate Sibo. He's young, cocky and he loves a pound note.

FRANKIE: I been praying so I destined to win.

GEORGE: The money's on you. MD's told me to bring the champagne.

FRANKIE: And if I lose?

GEORGE: You won't.

FRANKIE: If I do I won't get another go. So you better hope that these (*he holds his fist up*) house the Devil when so many deserve my attention. Don't worry none, some likkle white boy ain't gonna tek we, or stop them calling me champion.

The bell rings.

RING ANNOUNCER (V/O): Round one.

The projector shows actual archive footage.

GEORGE: Uncoil. Box not brawl. Keep it precise, contained.

FRANKIE: I'm holding on to what is right. No man can stop that, George.

The projector plays the last round of the fight.

We hear Harry Carpenter's commentary running over it.

The crowd is ecstatic.

George is just standing there.

GEORGE: Come on, Frankie, let's get out of here.

FRANKIE: Give me a minute.

GEORGE: Come on, Frankie.

FRANKIE: It's not them men there that make me a champion, George. It's my defeats. The fights that drag my will from the dark pit of my stomach to come back and beat a man or beat myself when all is equal.

GEORGE: You're fucking stoned, Frankie.

FRANKIE: It quietens the noise in my head, George.

GEORGE: Let's get out of here before I knock you spark out myself.

FRANKIE: God loves a tryer, George, you said that yourself.

GEORGE: No, Frankie. God, whoever he is, loves a winner

GEORGE leaves FRANKIE standing centre stage alone.

FRANKIE: Listen to that crowd roar. I just wanna soak it up. Feel the joy. Feel what I coulda been.

(Beat.)

If the game was fair but when the fight ain't fair boxing becomes your game of chess, George, and me move from king to pawn. But whatever the moves I am always a king, forever a king.

FRANKIE closes his eyes.

The lights come up on FRANKIE.

We hear cheers and the shouts of victory FRANKIE stands there awash with the atmosphere.

LIGHTS go down.

Gregory Isaac's Babylon Too Tough *plays.*

The projector reads 1980.

FRANKIE is sitting on the sofa smoking a spliff. He is playing with his cat.

FRANKIE turns the music down to listen to the radio. We hear the radio announce Minter will be fighting for the world title in Las Vegas against Vito Artuofermo for a record six-figure purse. John Conteh has retired and Frank Bruno is being trained by George Francis.

FRANKIE stops all noise, throws the cat off the sofa, and just looks. He gets up and starts to punch the air.

FRANKIE: They robbed me of everything, George. I need you to give me the courage of my defeats. One last fight, one last payday.

The projector shows: February 18th 1980, Frankie Lucas Vs Roy Gumbo World, Sporting Club Mayfair London, Southern Area Title.

FRANKIE is looking dejected, slumped in his corner. GEORGE is trying to get him up.

GEORGE: I've thrown in the towel, Frankie.

FRANKIE: Me more tired than hungry now, George.

GEORGE: I know. Come on, get up, let's go,

GEORGE helps FRANKIE up to walk him to his stool.

FRANKIE: This is all I've got.

GEORGE: I told you at the beginning to look after your Missus and Michael.

FRANKIE: You told me WE was a family. So how a man gonna be in two places at the same time, George?

GEORGE: I told you we were a brotherhood, that's different to family. Boxing has a short shelf-life. I do right by you, I play the game, I even try to change the game, but years ago a pal told me you gotta be like a doctor or a lawyer because boxers come and go, loving them will only bring grief.

FRANKIE: Did we change the game, George?

GEORGE: I like to think so but time will tell.

FRANKIE: Or we playing the same film with different actors?

GEORGE: Thinking like that can only bring grief.

FRANKIE: We ain't in the business of getting hurt?

GEORGE: We're both just men, Frankie. Doing the business the best we know how but that doesn't mean it don't get to break your heart.

GEORGE walks off thinking FRANKIE is behind him.

FRANKIE is alone in the ring and stares into the ether. He starts to punch at the air at an invisible foe.

Jimi Hendrix's Voodoo Child *plays.*

FRANKIE: Be gone.

And he does it all the way back to the sofa

The lights go out for a good second or two.

They come back up with KEN standing looking towards FRANKIE.

KEN: Come on, Frankie, open the door. It's me Ken and your Mum. Frankie, I know you're in there. Come out. If you don't open up I'll have to kick it in. Come on, everyone's worried about you.
Go on lads, kick it in but bring him out gently.

FRANKIE comes out with his left fist closed.

You're be OK, Frankie. They're taking you somewhere safe. To hospital.

FRANKIE just stares at KEN and puts his hands behind his back to be cuffed.

FRANKIE: Put back on the shackles.

KEN: How the hell did it get to this?

FRANKIE: The pebble

FRANKIE stares at KEN for a long second and slowly leaves.

The lights go down.

Silent pause then spotlight on GENE.

GENE: Mohammed Ali say it's not the mountain that wear a man down but the pebble in his shoe. They took Frankie to hospital but, after a while, he got a weekend pass. Say what you want but every Saturday without fail, he'd turn up looking for Michael. He'd arrive in a cab, come in, sit in the kitchen, look at Michael and say...

FRANKIE: Me was robbed, dem rob me. Me was robbed, dem rob me and... *(he spits.)*

GENE: Then he would call a cab to take him back. Frankie closed his left hand shut because he thought it housed the Devil, never to open it again.

GENE looks at FRANKIE who is sitting on the sofa and has his left arm tight against him, his hand behind his back. He is looking down.

GENE (CONTD): I guess in his mind he was protecting us. Protecting the world. And not one of them doctors or anyone else thought to help him release it, so now it's stuck so. Then just like that he stopped coming. Michael went to his flat to find it empty of the few things he loved: His records gone. His stereo gone and Ital him cat lying dead in the middle of the floor. There were the occasional sightings of him at Baker Street and Hampstead Heath and so on and so forth. But soon his name froze on people's lips until time melted he away and people thought him dead. Me and Michael knew Frankie was too damn hard ears to die. Especially when he'd been wronged so, but he was definitely out there all alone in the wilderness with nothing but his will to survive.

ACT 3

SCENE 1

Jimmy Cliff's Sitting in Limbo *plays.*

The action moves from the ring to the sofa and the ring has no light on it at all.

FRANKIE is sitting on the sofa, rolling spliffs even though his left arm is disabled and his fist still clenched shut.

GENE is sat to the side watching.

MICHAEL walks on stage from the far side and stands in front of the sofa and his Dad.

FRANKIE: Michael, Michael, that you?

MICHAEL: Yes, Daddy. It's me.

FRANKIE: Come, sit down.

MICHAEL sits and looks at FRANKIE, lighting his spliff and listening to the music playing. There is an awkward silence between them.

The music stops playing and the silence intensifies.

MICHAEL: Do you want some food?

FRANKIE: Me belly full.

MICHAEL: Some tea? I can ask the lady to bring you some.

FRANKIE: No please. You fetch me red Rizla? The big ones and some Malt loaf?

MICHAEL: Not red Rizla. I couldn't find them.

FRANKIE: I only want red.

MICHAEL: I couldn't find red.

FRANKIE: Go look until you do.

MICHAEL: It could take me all night and I'm here now.

FRANKIE: Go look for the red ones, Michael.

MICHAEL: You want me to leave?

FRANKIE: I want big red Rizla.

MICHAEL: Let me see if I can't find some here.

MICHAEL gets up and looks around in a drawer.

FRANKIE: You think I stupid? I tell ya I ain't got none.

MICHAEL finds some in the drawer and gives them to FRANKIE.

MICHAEL: They were stuck in the back. Not easy to see. Here you go.

FRANKIE: (*Grunts and throws the remote at MICHAEL*) Here YOU go. Choose some TV.

MICHAEL: I'm OK. You want I mek you some sweet tea and cut a piece of malt loaf for you?

FRANKIE: I want you to carry me downstairs for a smoke. After you roll me a few singles.

MICHAEL: How many singles?

FRANKIE: Ten.

MICHAEL: A marathon smoke then?

FRANKIE just watches him still in silence.

MICHAEL (CONTD): And that's ten. Come on. I'll take you down to the car.

FRANKIE: I can't be bothered to go downstairs. Open the window.

MICHAEL: You're not allowed.

FRANKIE: Just do as I tell ya. Look, close the door and open the window and put some music on.

Roy Ayers's Everyone loves the Sunshine *plays.*

FRANKIE passes Michael the spliff.

MICHAEL: Nah, thank you.

FRANKIE: It good for you.

MICHAEL takes the spliff and takes a toke and looks at his Dad staring out the window deep in music.

MICHAEL: Is it? You remember the sofa you used to have in that flat in Southampton Road?

FRANKIE: The blue leather one?

MICHAEL: I dunno why but the colour always reminded me of the sea. You would sit, smoking your herb, listening to the music and then you'd tell me to come over to sit with you.

FRANKIE: To listen to the radio together. And you would yam down the chocolate I had for you.

MICHAEL: And the crisps.

FRANKIE: Yes, yes. (*Smiles*) I remember teaching you to box. You still box?

MICHAEL: I did for a while.

FRANKIE: Orthodox or southpaw?

MICHAEL: Orthodox. But one time I change to southpaw to be like you, and it felt so different, like powerful and I was like, yeah, man, this is the lick. It felt dominant.

FRANKIE: (*Smiles and nods*) Why you stop?

MICHAEL: I was good but everyone knew I had a lot to live up to.

(*Beat.*)

What with you, you know, being a boxing legend.

FRANKIE: (*Looks surprised*) I am? (*He winks*)

MICHAEL: ...and I had trouble with my knee and Mummy didn't want it.

FRANKIE: You can't live your life for your Mummy.

MICHAEL: You forget how much getting punched hurts?

FRANKIE: No, I just remember how fantastic winning felt.

They both share a smile.

MICHAEL: (*Picks up the remote*) What you wanna watch?

FRANKIE: Boxing. Go ask the lady for some tea. Take these dirty plates with you. Mind to tell her please and thank you.

MICHAEL: I know, Daddy.

MICHAEL leaves and there is a moment of silence whilst FRANKIE just sits and waits.

MICHAEL comes back in with the clean plate and mug and puts them down and then sits next to his father.

You know they say you lost the Sibson fight because of this...

MICHAEL holds the spliff, looks at it before passing it back.

FRANKIE: I lost my cool.

MICHAEL: It looked like you had it til round five that is.

FRANKIE: Another bad decision against me.

MICHAEL: But he knock you down, Daddy. One punch done everything.

FRANKIE: He catch me with my chin out.

MICHAEL: Some say you he caught you off guard coz you were stoned.

FRANKIE: Not stoned enough.

MICHAEL: And dem say a lot of money made in your corner.

FRANKIE: Well, not a penny reach me.

MICHAEL: Mummy always said you came round with nothing but your long empty hands, but at least you bought yourself.

FRANKIE: And that was enough?

MICHAEL: Always.

FRANKIE: Til I didn't come.

(Beat.)

MICHAEL: Was that the "Wacky Baccy" too?

FRANKIE: No, that's because dem rob me.

MICHAEL: Of what?

FRANKIE: Of myself. Them make it so a man don't even have himself.

MICHAEL: Daddy, you remember Ken Rimmington?

FRANKIE: You foolish? If I remember Ken Rimmington.

MICHAEL: Well, it's his 60th Wedding anniversary and he having a party at him house and he want we go. The Mackenzies will be there, Tony Ray's son. It'll be like a reunion.

FRANKIE: I don't feel no reunion.

MICHAEL: It might be nice for you to see all those old faces

(Beat.)

FRANKIE: I said no.

MICHAEL: You remember when I was young you'd kneel down and we'd spar together? I loved boxing with you, watching you wink when I caught you with a little left hook, seeing how natural it felt to you. Like a second skin. How happy it made you. But there was one time when you catch me a little too hard and I spun across the room and landed under the Finnegan fight poster you had on the wall.

FRANKIE: I can't recall.

(Beat.)

MICHAEL: I saw the look of horror on your face. You came rushing over to see I was alright. But as you got to me I landed one hard punch right in your face and you fell back a step.

FRANKIE: They say the apple don't fall far from the tree.

MICHAEL: But once you saw it was all alright you laughed and then relaxed.

(Beat.)

We could go together.

FRANKIE: Where?

MICHAEL: To the party, see all your old boxing buddies.

(Beat.)

Relive that time. I'd come with you and, if you don't feel the joy, we'll leave.

FRANKIE: Be part of the uglies night out?

MICHAEL: But you're looking good Daddy, and besides I'll be with you.

FRANKIE: You'd stand with me?

MICHAEL: For sure. We man and son. Ain't that enough?

(Beat.)

FRANKIE: Always.

FADE TO BLACK.

SCENE 2

Lights come up on Ken's Office.

KEN is going through his desk and talking to himself.

KEN: Where's that bloody medal? I want the press to take a photo of it. It's what the club was all about. Ah, here it is.

KEN clasps it.

WE HEAR some chatter and music.

MICHAEL and FRANKIE walk in.

KEN: So glad you made it. It's nice to see you and Michael. He's done you proud. Lovely boy.

FRANKIE: Can you leave us alone a minute?

MICHAEL walks out.

He's a man.

KEN: Well, that may be but they're always our children no matter how big. Look sixty years married. And three children, nine grand children and 18 great grandchildren—don't ask me their names—and still in love.

He looks at a family photo on his shelf.

FRANKIE: 60 Years. Nice. You know for years I saw you as my father.

KEN: Thank you, Frankie. I still say with the right handling you could have gone all the way.

FRANKIE: As a boxer?

KEN: Yes. World Middleweight Champion.

FRANKIE: And as a man?

KEN: That part's yours alone, Frankie.

FRANKIE: So you just disappear?

KEN: No, we talked every now and then remember? And I came to some of your fights. I cared for you, still do, but I had a big day job, family too and then Bruce Baker took over the club because I got too busy for that as well. George was good. He had world champions for Christ sake, all coloured at a time when no one wanted any of you. I had to trust it and move on.

FRANKIE: And that's when I see us for what it was.

(Beat.)

I hear they try to do to Clinton what they did to me.

KEN: Yes, that's right. The 76 Olympics but when he applied to represent Jamaica they thought better of it and back-tracked.

They both chuckle.

FRANKIE: We mess them up then?

(Beat.)

KEN: A bit. Did you hear that George passed?

FRANKIE just looks at him.

FRANKIE: No, I'm sorry to hear that. Very sorry. When? How?

KEN: I'm not sure. I know he lost his wife and his son just before his passing. But what a legacy, ah, 42 titles.

(Beat.)

And those buggers still won't put him in the Boxing Hall of Fame.

FRANKIE: That his legacy. I remember a man who fought for what was right, A man whose legacy was breaking rules for what was fair. You know he made a living from boxing but he lived for his boxers.

KEN: Ay he did. He laid a lot of paving stones.

FRANKIE: All of us laid stones, Ken. Just some of us were the paving stones that got laid.

(Beat.)

You tell me "do as you're told" and you'll be fine. So I did but I wasn't.

KEN: When things went wrong I came as soon as I was called.

FRANKIE: But you didn't look for Michael.

KEN: I did what I could.

(Beat.)

FRANKIE: Dem mess me up. They send me from the hospital to home but no one check up on me or tend to my hand or help with my medicine so by the time I find me feet they quick come to put me back in hospital And then I made it so people couldn't find me.

KEN: Look, it' time you had this.

He grabs FRANKIE's good hand and places the medal in it.

I've kept it safe long enough. It belongs to you. You won it, against all the odds and you should have it.

FRANKIE looks at the medal in his hand and smiles.

FRANKIE: Back.

KEN: Huh?

FRANKIE: I should have it back. You forget it was me that give it to you. Thank you.

FRANKIE walks out of the office and calls to MICHAEL.

Michael we gone.

FADE TO BLACK.

SCENE 3

Lights come back up on GENE.

GENE: When I started seeing Frankie all those years ago, both my Mum and Frankie's Mum, told me not to bother with him. Stay away they said. He's trouble and trouble stains. But good job the young don't like to listen because Frankie taught me to carry on regardless. I mean even in the depths of his trouble he still came and brought his spirit with him. No matter what they put him... put us through. He never gave up. We never gave up. And lord knows what we ALL suffered back then. I mean, without Frankie there would be no Michael. Our gift to the world, our future. And look, when all is said and done, who else would be caring for Frankie now?

FRANKIE and MICHAEL are back on the sofa. Some time has passed, they are smoking.

MICHAEL: You miss the boxing?

FRANKIE: It's all I know, from when I was nine.

MICHAEL: You know you have to look hard to find any of your fights.

FRANKIE: Dem ghost me.

MICHAEL: Dem mek you dead. I heard the stories good and bad. Some horrible bad-mouth stories.

FRANKIE: Everybody got a mouth but not everyone know how to shut it.

MICHAEL: Is it true that you cried and left the room when Minter won the world title?

FRANKIE: I was a lion and dem make me a lamb.

MICHAEL: Not to me. You remember sometimes I would sit with you and you wouldn't say a word to me but you'd be talking in riddles, asking someone a question, even though there was no-one but us two and Ital in the room. You remember that time you punched a hole in the wall to kill the duppy.

FRANKIE: Before it reach you—and then you just left out. Somethings not for sharing I was so scared that when you went to the shop I split. And then your Mummy tell me that you didn't want to come by me no more.

MICHAEL: I left a note. But on the bus I realised that you wouldn't know what the fuck you were looking at and I started to feel real bad. I just wanted back on that 68 bus home.

FRANKIE: It's OK.

MICHAEL: But you just disappeared and for years I thought it was because of that note.

FRANKIE: In my mind it was for the best.

MICHAEL: All I knew was you were there one minute and gone the next but truthfully, I had so much love around me, it didn't make no dent and I don't mean that in a bad way.

FRANKIE: No bad way taken.

MICHAEL: I realise now that you were out there struggling on your own, but no one never discussed what was going on.

FRANKIE hands back the spliff to MICHAEL.

MICHAEL takes a tote, FRANKIE watches him.

FRANKIE: Like I said some things not for sharing but hear me good when I tell you that...

He takes the spliff...

this my friend and never my enemy

...and pulls on it.

MICHAEL: And then all we know you was in the hospital.

FRANKIE: And you come find me.

MICHAEL: Of course. I remember that first time seeing your hand clenched shut and dry, so dry it scaled up like fish scales. I thought you were some kind of Merman, and it must have dried out from all that salt you ate, like them dumplings you used to make, heavy like a snooker ball and harder than your head.

FRANKIE: Wot. You not like salt?

MICHAEL: But the mental stress must have...

FRANKIE: ...been heavier than them dumplings

(Beat.)

MICHAEL: You know Minter dead now, Daddy.

FRANKIE: 'im dead?

MICHAEL: He died last month. Tom in the trainer shop just told me. Cancer. Only 69. Tom said he didn't feel sad at all. First thing he did was ring his brother and they both shared a smile whilst paying respects.

FRANKIE: Why he hate him so?

MICHAEL: He said Minter belittled him one time when he had just lost a fight and Minter's words rested rent-free in his head for years.

FRANKIE: He hate him that easy?

MICHAEL: He hated what happened with Hagler but he bet it bought a smile to your face. The way Hagler pounded him and all the commotion after.

FRANKIE: Not really. We suffered that commotion at every fight. Minter just show the world England's true colours.

MICHAEL: Yeah. It saying something that Hagler never stepped foot here again.

(Beat.)

But I'm here, Daddy. We're here.

(Beat.)

Together. Even if most times we just sit in silence.

FRANKIE: Trust the silence, Michael. You don't wanna hear the noise in my head.

FRANKIE picks up a cup and plate.

Here, take this to she in the kitchen and be sure to smile and tell her thank you.

MICHAEL: I know, Daddy. You know you never thank me.

FRANKIE: Why? I a burden to you?

MICHAEL: No. This here, what we have between us, is a privilege.

FRANKIE: After the time that slipped between us? You know I'm sorry. Sorry I couldn't give you what I wanted for you.

MICHAEL: I didn't want for nothing, Daddy, and I trust the silence. I don't want to know anything that you don't want to tell me.

MICHAEL smiles. FRANKIE starts to show unrest so MICHAEL changes the subject.

I wish I could find more of your fights. Watch the wild man everyone was scared to fight, you at top form, full flow and slick What was it like winning the gold medal?

FRANKIE: Fantastic. Bloody fantastic.

MICHAEL: I bet, but it must have been lonely out there, just you.

FRANKIE: I went on a whole heap of hate but won on a lot of people's love.

MICHAEL: But it must have been hard.

FRANKIE sits up on the sofa and starts to ramble but not riddles—his clarity of thought—he talks to the ceiling not MICHAEL.

FRANKIE: Not as hard as hearing I wasn't going. That cruelty silenced my rage and knocked me for six, like I'd been shot then. I held my stomach tight, tight, tight, to stop all my hopes and dreams flooding out, carried away into a river of blood, washing the sorrow in the watchful eyes of the waiting, flowing far into tomorrow.

MICHAEL: Daddy?

MICHAEL brings him back.

But YOU WON, Daddy. Why didn't you keep the medal?

FRANKIE: It cost too dear. So much invested in the dream. I never promised you no big mansions or the stars and the moon. I just promise you would never know hunger or feel the cold alone. That your future would be free from cussing and fighting and as a father you could always look up to me. But them promises, them get robbed from me, like my promise as a man. And my hopes, which make all the toil and strife, the victories and defeats worth it, gone, as they tell me to focus on each fight and win. But the fights didn't come until I start losing and me never have no plan B.

MICHAEL: But I never did.

FRANKIE: Never did what?

MICHAEL: Go hungry or stand the cold alone.

FRANKIE: That your Mummy's doing.

MICHAEL: It's your sweetheart photos that she still carries on her phone. It takes two.

MICHAEL nudges FRANKIE.

FRANKIE: *(Smiling)* Of course.

(Beat.)

You know I went back home for a bit after New Zealand, but it couldn't hold me. It wasn't me yard no more.

MICHAEL: Why?

FRANKIE: Because your home here and my place with you.

FRANKIE starts to look for something.

MICHAEL: I got your smoke here, Daddy. Look I rolled you ten already.

FRANKIE: I not look for no smoke.

FRANKIE brings his hand around from behind his back.

I got this for you. Here take it. It's my legacy.

He places the medal in MICHAEL's hand.

It puts me at a place in time. It's what I can give you now.

MICHAEL: Thank you. I'll treasure this and the story behind it.

He holds the medal tight and looks at his Dad. Then he takes his wallet out and takes something out.

I got something for you too.

FRANKIE: You 'ave something for me?

(Beat.)

MICHAEL: I want you to know that I at peace with myself. For years I wanted more, always more, but these days I'm happy to just be. Somedays at work I have myself in hysterics, laugh out loud jokes, selling my cosmetics to pretty women that don't need them, some that do and to some women who want to believe they can get mermaid's hair from a bottle.

FRANKIE: Dem mermaids always give trouble.

Both laugh.

MICHAEL: I come here, I see Mummy and I'm grateful for my partner, my daughter and my grandson. For my life and the love I have in it. Everyday there is some kind of joy. You need to know that. Look take this.

He gives FRANKIE three photos. He looks at the top one.

The photos appear on the projector.

FRANKIE: I remember this. Me, Everard and Frank Bruno. Frank was just starting out and I took him to the gym.

MICHAEL: But look at you, so dapper, crisp and full of life. Look at your stance. Now look at me here in this photo.

FRANKIE: We like two peas in a pod. I just better looking.

MICHAEL: Always and look. See here my daughter. Look at her. See that smile, see the twinkle in her eye? Who that remind you of?

FRANKIE: Talking to her like talking to my Mummy.

MICHAEL: And look here. See my grandson, your great grandson? His pose, the wink, it's you, your energy. We may not have had the full father/son bonding thing but I always felt you loved me and look here in this photo.

He gives him the last photo.

Three generations together and the energy shines through. You see where we got it from.

They look at the photo and smile.

FRANKIE: Yeah, man.

MICHAEL: You know when I heard you had the cancer I got scared, so scared I would lose you again.

FRANKIE: You don't know boxers never like to give up.

MICHAEL: I know but it made me want to give you some kind of peace. We may have lost a few years but look what we gained. People search a lifetime to find their place and look at WE, right here, right here together, with those behind us and those in front.

They acknowledge each other.

Some things can't be robbed, Daddy.

FRANKIE: We still standing, like they say, you win some you lose some.

MICHAEL: But you live, Daddy. You live to fight another day.

FRANKIE: Always

Beat as they look at each other.

We can go in peace, Michael, because love can't pass. Come.

MICHAEL: Where?

FRANKIE: For a smoke, of course.

The projector shows: RIP Frankie Lucas.

Make It Break *by Sidders plays out.*

BLACKOUT

ALSO AVAILABLE FROM SALAMANDER STREET

All Salamander Street plays can be bought in bulk at a discount for performance or study. Contact info@salamanderstreet.com to enquire about performance licences.

CHICKEN BURGER N CHIPS by Corey Bovell

ISBN: 9781913630447

A raw and nostalgic coming of age story about growing up in South London.

KING HAMLIN by Gloria Williams

ISBN: 9781739103033

A touching and engrossing story of friendship between three youngsters against the harsh reality of knife crime and gang culture in London.

LAMENT FOR SHEKU BAYOH by Hannah Lavery

ISBN: 9781914228230

Based upon the true story of a death in custody, *Lament for Sheku Bayoh* asks the urgent question, is Scotland really a safe place?

NOWHERE by Khalid Abdalla

ISBN: 9781068696251

Khalid Abdalla's surprising solo show about his own history and involvement in the Egyptian revolution of 2011.rd.

OUTLIER by Malaika Kegode

ISBN: 9781914228339

Genre-defying and emotional, *Outlier* is a powerful play exploring the impact of isolation, addiction and friendship on young people in the often-forgotten places.

PLACEHOLDER by Catherine Bisset

ISBN: 9781914228919

A dramatic solo play set in 1790 Saint Domingue—the daughter of an enslaved woman reflects on her life as an opera singer and the importance of resistance.